HIGH BLOOD PRESSURE

What You Need to Know

Johns Hopkins Editors

Lawrence Appel, M.D.
Associate Professor of Medicine, Epidemiology,
and International Health
The Johns Hopkins University School of Medicine

Robert McNamara, M.D., M.S.
Instructor, Epidemiology
The Johns Hopkins University School of Hygiene and Public Health

Jerilyn K. Allen, Sc.D.
Associate Professor of Nursing
The Johns Hopkins University School of Nursing

Editorial Director
Laura J. Wallace

Writer
Mark Giuliucci

Johns Hopkins Office of Consumer Health Information
Ron Sauder, Director
Molly L. Mullen, Editor

Johns Hopkins USA assists out-of-town patients with any aspect of arranging a visit to the Johns Hopkins Medical Institutions—from scheduling appointments to providing guidance on hotels, transportation, and preferred routes of travel. The program has up-to-date information on clinical practices and is a resource center for maps, visitor guides, and other materials of interest to non-local patients. Client Services Coordinators in the Johns Hopkins USA offices are available Monday through Friday from 8:30 a.m. until 5:00 p.m. (Eastern). They can be reached toll-free at 1-800-507-9952 or locally at 410-614-USA1. You can also visit Johns Hopkins on the World Wide Web at *http://hopkins.med.jhu.edu/*.

Johns Hopkins
HEALTH

HIGH BLOOD PRESSURE

What You Need to Know

TIME
LIFE
BOOKS

Alexandria, Virginia

The information in this book is for your general knowledge only. It is not intended as a substitute for the advice of a physician. You should seek prompt medical care for any specific health problems you may have.

Time-Life Books is a division of Time Life Inc.

Time Life Inc.
President and CEO: George Artandi

Time-Life Custom Publishing
Vice President and Publisher: Terry Newell
Vice President of Sales and Marketing: Neil Levin
Director of Special Sales: Liz Ziehl
Editor for Special Markets: Anna Burgard

Published by Ottenheimer Publishers, Inc.
5 Park Center Court, Suite 300
Owings Mills, MD 21117-5001
JH004M L K J I H G F E D C B A

First printing. Printed and bound in U.S.A. M L K J I H G F E D C B A

Time-Life is a trademark of Time Warner Inc. U.S.A.

ISBN: 0-7370-1610-8

Library of Congress Cataloging-in-Publication Data
Giuliucci, Mark.
    High blood pressure : what you need to know / by Mark Giuliucci.
        p.   cm. — (Johns Hopkins health)
    ISBN 0-7370-1610-8 (pbk. : alk. paper)
    1. Hypertension Popular works.   I. Title.   II. Series.
RC685.H8G53   1999
616.1'32—dc21   99-26954
                                                                  CIP

Books produced by Time-Life Custom Publishing are available at special bulk discounts for promotional and premium use. Custom adaptations can also be created to meet your specific marketing goals. Call 1-800-323-5255.

CONTENTS

INTRODUCTION

Doctors call high blood pressure the silent killer. That's because most people with the condition feel no symptoms, except for maybe an occasional headache. Unlike pneumonia, a broken hip, or arthritis, high blood pressure can quietly linger in the body—sometimes for decades—before being detected.

All the while, it can do serious damage. High blood pressure is one of the leading causes of heart disease and strokes and can harm your kidneys, eyes, and other organs as well. Though it's hard to be sure, researchers believe that high blood pressure leads to more than 700,000 deaths in the United States each year.

Fortunately, the word is finally getting out about the silent killer. Thanks to better screening, better education, and better treatment, the number of Americans with high blood pressure has dropped by more than eight million since the early 1970s. Because more and more people are learning to control their blood pressure, the risk of dying from a stroke or a heart attack has dropped by more than 50 percent over the past two decades.

While high blood pressure often can't be cured, lifestyle changes, such as diet, exercise, and medication, almost always work to control it. Chances are you won't need years of treatment to begin seeing the benefits, either, because even the smallest drop in blood pressure can greatly improve your chances of avoiding harm.

There are many ways to lower high blood pressure. It may mean cutting back on salt, eating more vegetables, reading food labels more closely, and taking an after-dinner walk instead of an after-dinner drink. You may need to take a pill once or twice a day, too. However, these minor changes are a small price to pay for the years they can add to your life.

Of course, the easiest way to avoid the dangers of high blood pressure is to never develop it in the first place. Doctors now know that blood pressure doesn't automatically rise as you get older—especially if you take good care of yourself. No matter what your age, sex, race, or ethnic background, steps you take now can help keep your blood pressure in check for the rest of your life.

If you already have high blood pressure, please use this book as a guide to help you through your diagnosis and treatment. You'll find up-to-the-minute information on diet, exercise, drugs, and everything else you'll need to get your pressure down. You'll find easy-to-read charts and graphs on which foods to add to your diet, how much salt is too much, which kinds of workouts may work out best for you, which medications may help you most, and which kinds of over-the-counter drugs may interfere with your treatment. While this book is by no means intended to replace your doctor's care and advice, it can be a great supplement to your treatment. Remember, *you* are the person most responsible for your own well-being. The more you know, the better off you'll be.

If you have a spouse, relative, or friend with high blood pressure, this book can help you help them. They'll be running into technical terms and treatments that they've never heard of before. They may become confused about medications, unsure of their choices in treatment, or just plain scared of what may happen. Nothing eases the mind of a concerned patient more than a caring, informed partner.

And finally, if you and your family have been lucky enough to avoid high blood pressure so far, please use this book as an ounce of prevention. Survey results show that nearly 13 percent of the adults in the United States—a total of about 50 million—have blood pressure readings that are within a few points of hypertension. If you take steps now to lower your blood pressure even the slightest bit, it can make all the difference in the world. Researchers believe that we could reduce the number of cases of hypertension by 20 to 50 percent if people with borderline readings would do what they need to do now, instead of waiting until things get out of control.

It's never too early to develop good eating habits. It's not too soon to educate yourself, your children, or your parents about proper exercise. The more you know about the detection and treatment of high blood pressure, the more likely you'll be to avoid the silent killer altogether. What you start doing today can make a difference for the rest of your life.

The Johns Hopkins University (including its world-renowned Schools of Medicine, Nursing, and Public Health) and the closely related Johns Hopkins Health Systems are well known for their commitment to medical research, education, and patient care. For the past eight years, The Johns Hopkins Hospital has been ranked the number one hospital in the United States in an annual survey conducted by *U.S. News and World Report.* In this book, Johns Hopkins presents a comprehensive, clearly written guide to preventing and controlling high blood pressure. When it comes to health advice, you want expert knowledge and compassionate guidance, and that's precisely what you'll find here. The information in this book is based on the latest research and the years of experience of the finest health professionals anywhere. You can be assured that what you read within these pages is information you can trust and just what you need at your side in your fight against high blood pressure.

High Blood Pressure: What It Is, What It Does

The next time you go to a ball game, hop on a bus, or stop by your favorite restaurant, take a look around. For every 20 people you see, chances are that 5 have blood pressure readings that are too high.

All told, more than 50 million American adults have high blood pressure (also called hypertension). That makes it the most widespread health problem in the country today. While you may not hear as much about it, hypertension affects more people than cancer, diabetes, arthritis, or AIDS. And every year, another 2 million people will develop high blood pressure for the first time.

Why is high blood pressure so common? Doctors say it's a combination of who we are, what we eat, and how we live. Genetics, diet, and lifestyle all affect our bodies—and the wrong mix can really put the squeeze on the circulatory system, which is where high blood pressure gets its start.

Blood pressure constantly rises and falls during the day. When you sleep, for instance, your body processes slow down, and your blood pressure dips. That's because blood's main job is to carry oxygen and nutrients to all of your cells.

HITCH A RIDE ON THE BLOODMOBILE

Your body is made up of nearly 100 trillion cells—and every one of them needs to eat. They demand oxygen, sugars, water, and hundreds of other nutrients every minute of every day. Talk about mouths to feed!

The job of providing all of this nourishment falls to your blood. Adults have a little more than a gallon of blood in their bodies, and it's filled with the stuff of life. Blood carries oxygen, glucose (a form of sugar), water, and proteins. It also contains white blood cells, which fight disease, and platelets, which help stop bleeding and repair cuts.

Blood travels through an amazingly complex network of arteries, veins, and capillaries. In fact, your body contains about 60,000 miles of these elastic tubes. That's 50 percent more miles than the entire U.S. interstate highway system—enough distance to circle the equator two and a half times.

Different blood vessels do different jobs. Arteries carry fresh blood (loaded with oxygen) away from your heart and toward your body's needy cells. Veins carry blood back to your heart and lungs for an oxygen refill. Vessels range in size from the giant aorta, which carries blood from the heart down the trunk of your body, to tiny capillaries. These miniature vessels feed individual cells and are barely large enough to permit a single red blood cell to squeeze through.

Of course, blood won't go anywhere without some help. That's where your heart comes in. The heart is a super-strong, pulsing muscle that squeezes blood in and out more than 60 times a minute. Its main job is to create pressure in the arteries, pressure that pushes blood along and helps keep your body running.

It's a little bit like the plumbing in your house. A pump brings water up from the well. The water fills the pipes in your house, creating pressure in the system. When you open a faucet, pressure pushes the water into your drinking glass, bathtub, or garden hose—wherever you need it. So a little blood pressure isn't a bad thing at all. In fact, your blood wouldn't go anywhere without it. Your cells wouldn't get fed. Your brain wouldn't get oxygen. In short, you wouldn't be you.

When there's less demand for these things, your heart and blood vessels can afford to relax a little. Your body is very efficient and never works harder than it has to.

When you take a brisk walk, however, things quickly change. Your muscles are working overtime, and they need help to keep going. Blood pressure rises to meet the demand. You breathe harder to get more oxygen into your lungs, your lungs transport the oxygen into the bloodstream, and then your arteries take the oxygen to the places your body needs it most.

Your blood pressure even changes when you do something as simple as standing up from a chair. If you've been seated for a while, blood has collected in your lower legs. When you stand up, your brain detects the change in position and responds by raising blood pressure to get that blood in your legs back in circulation.

How does the body raise and lower blood pressure? Actually, several different things can do it. First is the heart. It reacts to demands from your body by beating faster or slower. If you're resting, your heart will take it easy. If you're exercising—or if you have a sudden scare, such as a strange dog growling and running at you—your heart goes to work in a hurry.

PRESSURE POINTS

Your body adjusts blood pressure in three main ways:

1) The heart can change the rate and force at which it beats. The harder and faster it pumps, the higher your blood pressure rises.

2) The small arteries, called arterioles, can change their size. When they constrict and narrow, up goes your blood pressure.

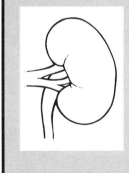

3) The kidneys can change the amount of water they keep in the bloodstream. The more water, the higher your blood pressure. Kidneys do this by increasing or reducing the amount of sodium in the body. In addition, kidneys produce renin, which can produce hormones that constrict blood vessels and cause the body to retain more sodium.

The kidneys also play a role in regulating blood pressure. They determine how much fluid stays in the blood and how much gets pumped out of the body in the urine. If the kidneys leave more fluid in the bloodstream, the result is more blood. More blood trying to squeeze through arteries and veins means higher blood pressure. But if the kidneys take more fluid out of the bloodstream, the volume of blood goes down—and so does pressure.

Blood vessels themselves can affect blood pressure, too. Unlike the copper pipes in your house, arteries are flexible. They are lined with smooth muscle tissue and can expand or contract. When the smooth muscle contracts, the arteries narrow and blood pressure increases. That's because the same amount of blood is trying to squeeze through a smaller opening. On the other hand, when the smooth muscle relaxes, arteries widen and blood pressure drops.

Blood pressure changes are controlled by special nerves called baroreceptors. They are located in the kidneys and blood vessels. When triggered, they tell the kidneys and arteries to raise or lower pressure. Just how they deliver this message gets a little complicated. Several hormones have powerful effects on blood pressure. Three hormones— renin, angiotensin, and aldosterone—work together to regulate blood pressure. Renin comes mainly from the kidneys. When it enters the bloodstream, it searches out angiotensinogen, a special protein that's made mainly by your liver. These two substances react to form angiotensin I. This new compound then works its way through the blood to the lungs. Once in the lungs, angiotensin I gets converted to a new, powerful hormone called angiotensin II.

Angiotensin II can raise blood pressure in two ways. First, it can signal the blood vessels to contract. Second, it can flow back to the kidneys and control how much salt and water the blood holds and how much is excreted. It does this by stimulating the kidneys to produce the hormone aldosterone, which makes the kidneys hold on to sodium (salt). By controlling salt, the kidneys also control the amount of fluid in the bloodstream. Remember, the more water in the blood, the higher the volume—and the higher the pressure. But to reduce pressure, don't restrict your water intake. Salt is the culprit. Water just comes along for the ride.

Some high blood pressure medications, such as ACE (angiotensin-converting enzyme) inhibitors and angiotensin II receptor blockers, work by controlling these hormones at different points in the process. We'll talk much more about medications in chapter 5.

Adrenaline and noradrenaline are powerful hormones, released at nerve endings and by the adrenal gland. These hormones, also termed the "stress hormones," can raise blood pressure abruptly, often in stressful situations such as public speaking. A class of medicine called beta-blockers controls blood pressure by thwarting the effects of these hormones.

Nitric oxide is a "local" hormone that also controls blood pressure. It's produced in the walls of your arteries and is made from an amino acid called L-arginine. Nitric oxide works by causing your blood vessels to widen. But researchers have found that in some people, the body isn't able to convert L-arginine into nitric oxide. This means your blood vessels will tend to stay tight, causing your blood pressure to rise. Right now, no one is sure why this happens.

As you get older, it can be normal for your blood vessels to release less nitric oxide. This means that your arteries will have a tougher time relaxing, even if you don't actually have hypertension.

WHAT'S EVERYBODY SO PUMPED UP ABOUT?

What's so bad about high blood pressure? Plenty. Your heart, kidneys, and other organs, as well as your blood vessels, simply aren't designed to handle constant pressure. They need to relax at lower pressure levels to stay healthy.

Over time, hypertension can lead to serious health problems, including the following:

Stroke. Hypertension is the leading cause of stroke. That's because high blood pressure can cause atherosclerosis (also known as hardening of the arteries), a condition in which sticky stuff called plaque attaches itself to the inside walls of arteries and slows the flow of blood. Doctors aren't quite sure how this happens. They believe that high blood pressure might injure the cells that line your arteries. This may lead to chemical reactions that make the cholesterol flowing through your blood attach to artery walls. Over time, this can cause plaque deposits.

When an artery feeding your brain gets too narrow because of plaque, you're at risk of what's called an ischemic stroke, in which a blood clot gets stuck in the narrowed section of the blood vessel. Suddenly, blood can't flow to the brain. Without blood, brain cells can't get oxygen and may start to die. A full-blown ischemic stroke can be fatal.

A burst blood vessel in the brain can cause a very serious type of stroke called a hemorrhagic stroke. Unlike an ischemic stroke, which is caused by a blockage, a hemorrhagic stroke occurs when blood from the broken artery spills into the brain, causing pressure to build up in the skull. This can deprive parts of the brain of vital oxygen. The result can be irreversible brain damage. People with hypertension are far more likely to suffer hemorrhagic strokes than people with normal blood pressure.

People with hypertension also are more likely to experience transient ischemic attacks, or mini-strokes. These are like ischemic strokes, except that the blockage either isn't complete or eventually opens up. While not always as serious as ischemic strokes, mini-strokes can cause permanent

BLOOD PRESSURE AND STROKES

High blood pressure is the number one risk factor for strokes. About 70 percent of all strokes are caused by hypertension. There are two main types of strokes. Ischemic strokes are caused by blood clots that block blood supply to the brain. Hemorrhagic strokes, which are less common, occur when blood vessels in the brain rupture. Fortunately, the risk of having either type of stroke can be lowered by controlling your blood pressure.

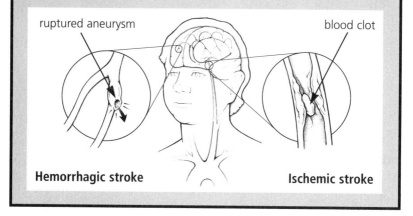

ruptured aneurysm

blood clot

Hemorrhagic stroke

Ischemic stroke

damage to the brain over time. Depending on where the blockage occurs, you could lose control over parts of your body, have difficulty with speech, or develop any number of other problems.

Coronary heart disease. The same plaque that blocks arteries to the brain can clog arteries that feed the heart. Remember that all cells need oxygen from the bloodstream to survive. So reducing the amount of blood to the heart muscle can drastically weaken it. If a blood clot gets stuck in one of these heart arteries (called coronary arteries), heart muscle cells can die. This is a heart attack.

When too many heart muscle cells die, or when the heart muscle has been strained for a long time, the heart can't pump blood through the body very well. This is called heart failure. Obviously, both a heart attack and heart failure are extremely serious and sometimes fatal.

Hypertension also increases your chances of developing an irregular heartbeat. One type of irregular heartbeat is called atrial fibrillation. This jumpy heartbeat can force a blood clot out of the heart and into the body. If the clot finds its way to the brain, it can cause a stroke. Men with high blood pressure are 50 percent more likely to develop atrial fibrillation than men with normal pressure. Women with high blood pressure have a 40 percent greater risk than women with normal pressure.

Kidney damage. Your kidneys are responsible for removing excess fluid and waste from your body. They work by filtering the blood that passes through them. But high blood pressure can damage the arteries within the kidneys. It can also narrow the arteries that feed blood to the kidneys. Either way, the kidneys become less efficient at removing fluid and waste. The worst-case scenario is called renal failure—a complete shutdown of kidney function. When this happens, you need dialysis or a kidney transplant.

High blood pressure can be double trouble where your kidneys are concerned. If you have hypertension, you might suffer kidney damage and reduced kidney function. This, in turn, can lead to even higher blood pressure, since your kidneys won't be able to remove excess fluid from the bloodstream. This is why controlling high blood pressure is so important. It breaks the vicious circle of damage.

Aneurysm. Constant high blood pressure puts quite a strain on your arteries. It can cause them to develop bulges that balloon out and weaken over time. Sometimes these bulges—called aneurysms—burst, causing drastic problems. When the burst blood vessel is in the brain, the result is a hemorrhagic stroke, which we talked about earlier. Another type of aneurysm involves the aorta, the huge artery that carries blood from the heart down the chest and into your midsection. Over time, extra pressure can weaken this vital artery and cause it to burst. In especially bad cases, the weak spot can actually split the walls of the aorta—a condition known as a dissecting aortic aneurysm. This type of aneurysm causes tremendous pain in your chest, abdomen, or back.

Lowering blood pressure can reduce your chances of developing an aneurysm. If you already have one, you may need surgery to repair it. If the aneurysm is small, your doctor may just monitor it to make sure it doesn't increase in size and require an operation to fix.

Left ventricular hypertrophy. Everyone wants a strong heart. But sometimes it can grow too strong for its own good.

When your blood pressure rises, your heart must work extra hard to pump blood. The heart reacts by growing bigger—just as your biceps would if you started lifting weights.

Unfortunately, bigger isn't better where your heart is concerned. If the heart wall grows too large, it reduces the space inside your left ventricle (that's the chamber within the heart that pumps blood into the bloodstream). This condition is known as left ventricular hypertrophy.

The enlarged heart muscle now needs additional blood to keep itself healthy. But because hypertension can lead to hardening of the arteries—especially the arteries in the heart itself—the muscle sometimes can't get enough blood.

The heart then becomes weaker, not stronger, since it can't feed itself properly.

The result is a host of problems, ranging from chest pain called angina to irregular heartbeats, heart attack, and heart failure. Left ventricular hypertrophy occurs more often in men and overweight people, both of whom are more prone to heart disease to begin with. But when women develop the disorder, the results can be deadly. Researchers have discovered that women with left ventricular hypertrophy may be four times more likely to die of any cause (even those not related to heart problems) than women without the condition.

Reducing high blood pressure may stop dangerous growth of the heart muscle and may even reduce the muscle's size. So it's essential that you work to lower your pressure to avoid further problems from left ventricular hypertrophy.

Eye damage. Your eyes are very sensitive to hypertension, since they have extremely fine arteries feeding blood to them. Left unchecked, high blood pressure can greatly damage these delicate blood vessels. The walls of the arteries grow thicker so that they can handle the additional pressure from the bloodstream. This, in turn, causes the arteries to narrow. When this happens, blockages can occur—or the arteries may hemorrhage, causing blood to leak into the eyes. Either way, this can harm the optic nerves and cause partial loss of vision.

The higher your blood pressure and the longer it's left untreated, the higher the possibility of eye damage. Fortunately, lowering your pressure can actually help reverse some of the harm. Be sure to tell your eye doctor about your condition, so he can monitor your eyes for signs of damage.

A REAL BRAIN-BUSTER

High blood pressure may affect your mind as well as your body. The famous Framingham Heart Study (which has been studying the health of more than 5,000 residents of Framingham, Massachusetts, for several decades) showed that people with hypertension often suffered a loss of brain functions such as memory over a 20-year period. Another study of 8,000 Japanese-American men showed that the higher their blood pressure, the higher their risk of losing abilities such as concentration, judgment, abstract thought, and short- and long-term memory.

Doctors believe that these losses may be caused by the same culprit that causes so many other problems: damaged blood vessels. If the arteries that lead to the brain suffer long-term injury from high blood pressure, they simply can't deliver enough oxygen and food there. The brain may then lose nerve cells in places that are responsible for these various functions.

PRIMARY HYPERTENSION

There are two types of high blood pressure: primary hypertension and secondary hypertension. The great majority of people with high blood pressure—more than 95 in every 100—have primary hypertension, which used to be called essential hypertension.

While doctors know how primary hypertension develops, they don't always know why. In truth, physicians can almost never tell you exactly what caused your hypertension. That's really not unusual in medicine; there are several medical conditions—including cancer—for which finding a clear cause is difficult.

But doctors have identified a number of things that make you more likely to develop primary hypertension. These are called risk factors. They include:

High sodium intake. There's little doubt that too much sodium, or salt (which, chemically speaking, is sodium chloride), can have a powerful effect on blood pressure. Most of us eat way too much salt every day. In truth, your body hardly needs any salt to function properly.

Water and sodium work together. The more salt that you eat, the more sodium that winds up in your kidneys. And when there's too much sodium present, the kidneys leave more water in the bloodstream. This increases the overall volume of blood in the bloodstream and raises blood pressure.

For some unknown reason, sodium doesn't affect everyone equally. Some people are more sensitive than others to its pressure-raising effects. Since it's tough to tell who's sensitive to sodium, it's a good idea for everybody to cut down.

Obesity. Overweight people are two to six times more likely to develop high blood pressure. In fact, 4 of every 10 people with high blood pressure are overweight. That's a very strong connection.

The good news is that you don't have to lose much weight to reduce blood pressure. Dropping as few as 5 to 10 pounds can greatly lower your risk of developing hypertension—or even control hypertension if you already have it.

Family history. If a relative has high blood pressure, you're at higher risk for developing the disease, too. You may have inherited your mother's nose—and your father's hypertension problems.

It's unclear whether genetics is the main reason that high blood pressure runs in families. It could be that your environment—including the foods you learned to eat—is more important. Still, researchers believe they have found at least three genes in which flaws or mutations can make someone more likely to develop hypertension. One of the genes controls the production and release of the hormone angiotensin I, which has a direct effect on blood pressure. Another controls aldosterone, which also alters blood pressure. And the third plays a role in how much water your blood retains. Again, the more water in the blood, the greater the volume—and the higher your blood pressure. Of course, there's nothing you can do to change your family tree. Scientists are trying to figure out how to alter genes to make them work properly, but a solution will be years if not decades away. So if there is hypertension in your family, you should be even more on the alert than most people. Make sure you closely follow the guidelines in this book—including suggestions for the foods you eat, the exercise you need, and the medicine you take. The changes you make could mean the difference between normal and high blood pressure.

Poor diet. Many of us take in way too many salty foods and way too few important nutrients. There's evidence, for example, that those who don't get enough potassium may put themselves at risk for developing high blood pressure. That's because potassium helps blood vessels relax and may help get rid of sodium, too.

Other things we eat and drink affect blood pressure, too. Caffeine raises blood pressure in the short term, although its long-term effects aren't clear. Many scientific studies show that drinking excess alcohol can also raise blood pressure.

Syndrome X. This scary-sounding problem is really a combination of risk factors: obesity, high levels of triglycerides in your bloodstream, low levels of "good" HDL cholesterol, and early development of heart disease. Researchers have discovered that people with this group of health problems are more likely to develop high blood pressure. The trouble starts when you become over-weight—especially if you carry the extra body fat across your abdomen.

Diabetes. Syndrome X risk factors can also set the stage for diabetes, a dangerous buildup of blood sugar.

High blood pressure often accompanies diabetes. This is because diabetes can damage your kidneys and cause them to retain water. It also makes your nervous system more active, which can lead to hypertension, too. More than three million Americans have both diabetes and high blood pressure. In fact, if you have diabetes, you're about twice as likely to get hypertension as people who don't.

These two diseases can be a dangerous mix. Each is a major risk factor for heart disease, and the combination of the two is doubly damaging. Plus, 35 to 75 percent of all complications from diabetes are caused by high blood pressure. For this reason, many experts believe that people with diabetes should receive more aggressive treatment for their high blood pressure than other folks. In fact, new guide-lines suggest that people with diabetes should be treated with medication when their blood pressure reaches only the high-normal range. Normally, people with blood pressure in this range don't start drug therapy.

African-Americans are about twice as likely as whites to develop diabetes and hypertension together. The risk is even higher for Mexican-Americans—they are three times more likely than non-Hispanic whites to have both conditions.

Stress. Most people assume there's a strong connection between stress and blood pressure. But the evidence is not consistent. The Framingham Heart Study suggests that men between ages 45 and 59 have a greater risk of hypertension if they also show signs of high anxiety. Other studies have concluded that people in lower socioeconomic groups, who may tend to experience more stress, develop high blood pressure more often than those in other groups. Still, some studies show no link between stress and blood pressure.

If you have any one of the risk factors described above, your chances of developing high blood pressure will go up. If you start combining factors—say, obesity and high sodium intake, or high sodium intake and family history—your chances will increase even more. That's why it's so important to start reducing your risk factors now, before they get out of control and your blood pressure starts to rise.

SECONDARY HYPERTENSION

Now let's move on to the other kind of high blood pressure: secondary hypertension. Unlike primary hypertension, which often has mysterious origins, secondary hypertension is caused by identifiable problems somewhere else in your body. These problems include:

Kidney trouble. Again, the main job of your kidneys is to remove waste and excess water from the bloodstream. They do this by filtering the blood and creating urine. But when there's a disease in the kidneys, they can't work as well as they should. In many cases, blood flow to one or both kidneys drops because the arteries leading to them become too narrow. When the kidneys detect that they're not getting enough blood, they put more renin into the bloodstream. Renin, remember, is a hormone that helps raise blood pressure. By raising blood pressure, the kidneys are trying to get more blood so that they can work better. Of course, the higher blood pressure doesn't do any good for the rest of the body. This condition is known as renovascular hypertension.

Coarctation of the aorta. The aorta is the giant artery that feeds blood directly from the heart to the lower body. In a condition called coarctation, there's an abrupt narrowing of the aorta at some point in the chest. To get blood through this opening, the heart has to pump harder. This raises blood pressure at points in your body that are above the narrowed part of the aorta. Blood pressure below the narrowed opening is normal or even low.

Hypertension in children is not common. But when a child does have high blood pressure, it may be due to a narrowed aorta. Over time, a child's aorta may grow large enough to work properly—but sometimes surgery is needed to correct the problem.

Adrenal tumors. Your adrenal glands are located on top of the kidneys. They release hormones that control everything from sexual function to food digestion. When an abnormal growth, called a tumor, occurs on one of the glands, it can cause a variety of changes in the body—including increased blood pressure.

A tumor on the outer layer (the cortex) of the adrenal gland can lead to a condition called aldosteronism. Aldosterone is the hormone that signals the kidneys to leave water in the bloodstream. When there's a tumor on the adrenal gland, it may produce far too much aldosterone. Too much aldosterone means too much water in the blood. This increases the overall volume of blood, causing blood pressure to rise.

People with Cushing's syndrome have a different kind of tumor on the outer layer of one or both of the adrenal glands. This tumor causes the release of extra cortisone, a hormone that can also raise blood pressure.

A tumor on the inner part (the medulla) of the adrenal gland, on the other hand, can lead to excess adrenaline and noradrenaline in the bloodstream. These two hormones can have powerful effects on blood pressure. They're the same hormones that make your heart race when you are frightened. Imagine how hard your heart would work if your body was tricked into constantly feeling as though a Bengal tiger were chasing you!

In some cases, surgeons can remove adrenal tumors, and the glands begin to function normally again. The medulla region of the adrenal gland can usually be removed altogether without too much effect on the rest of the body.

Hormone problems. Other glands in your body also release hormones that indirectly affect blood pressure. Your pituitary gland may release too much growth hormone. Your thyroid gland might create too much (or too little) of its hormones. Or a tumor on the parathyroid gland may be the culprit. If you have high blood pressure, your doctor may screen you for malfunctions in all of these areas if she thinks you may have secondary hypertension.

Drug reactions. Sometimes taking the "wrong" pill can lead to hypertension. There are thousands of drugs in the world today. For some people, even common medications may create imbalances in the blood system that cause blood pressure to rise.

Over-the-counter drugs such as nasal decongestants, diet pills, and cold formulas can raise blood pressure. These drugs may also interfere with medications that you're already taking to control hypertension. If you have high blood pressure, read labels before taking any new drugs. Better yet, check with your doctor or pharmacist.

There's some evidence that a type of everyday painkiller can lead to blood pressure problems. These drugs are known as nonsteroidal anti-inflammatory drugs, or NSAIDs. Common NSAIDs include indomethacin (Indocin is one common brand), ibuprofen (Advil or Motrin), and naproxen (Aleve). (Another NSAID is aspirin, but it hasn't been linked to problems with blood pressure.) People often take these medications on a regular basis to help deal with arthritis or other causes of chronic pain. While the pills apparently don't raise blood pressure immediately, they may have a long-term impact. One study of men and women over age 65 revealed that those taking NSAIDs were as much as 90 percent more likely to eventually need high blood pressure medication. The risk was highest for those who took especially high doses or who took medication for one to three months. (This does not mean that arthritis sufferers should stop taking their medicine, however.)

A number of prescription drugs can also raise blood pressure or interfere with blood pressure medications. These drugs include antidepressants such as venlafaxine, cyclosporine, corticosteroids, erythropoietin, and MAO (monoamine oxidase) inhibitors. Be sure to remind your doctor about your high blood pressure before starting any new medication.

Controlled substances—particularly cocaine and amphetamines—can also raise blood pressure. Obviously, these drugs have other serious effects on the body, too.

For a more complete list of drugs that could aggravate your hypertension, see pages 170-171.

NOT ONLY FOR MEN

About one in four American adults has hypertension. But the number isn't equally divided among people of different ages and races. And while about the same percentage of men and women develop high blood pressure, they often get it at different times in their lives.

For example, men are far more likely to get high blood pressure earlier in life. Between ages 30 and 39, about 9 percent of Mexican-American men have high blood pressure. The figure for white men in this age group is 13 percent, and for African-American men, it is about 21 percent.

Meanwhile, less than 5 percent of white women between ages 18 and 49 have high blood pressure. For African-American women, the figure is about 11 percent, and for Mexican-American women it's 6 percent. As you can see, these figures are about half as high as the figures for men. Doctors aren't entirely sure why women in this age bracket have a lower risk of hypertension. Some experts believe that it could have something to do with female hormones such as estrogen, which women produce in great quantity until menopause. Estrogen appears to help protect most women from heart disease prior to menopause—but after that, all bets are off.

Between ages 50 and 59, hypertension rates soar for both sexes. About 42 percent of white men, 36 percent of Mexican-American men, and 56 percent of African-American men in this age group have blood pressure readings that are higher than normal. Among women in this age group, the figures are 37 percent for whites, 34 percent for Mexican-Americans, and 48 percent for African-Americans.

By age 70, women's readings actually surpass men's. Sixty-seven percent of white women, 73 percent of African-

PERCENTAGE OF PEOPLE WITH HYPERTENSION BY AGE AND POPULATION						
AGE	PERCENTAGE WITH HYPERTENSION					
	African-American		Mexican-American		White	
	Men	Women	Men	Women	Men	Women
30-39	21	11	9	6	13	5
50-59	56	48	36	34	42	37
70-79	68	73	52	67	60	67
(Source: Third National Health and Nutrition Examination Survey)						

American women, and 67 percent of Mexican-American women over age 70 have high blood pressure readings. For men, the figures are 60 percent for white men, 52 percent for Mexican-American men, and 68 percent for African-American men. These rates include persons whose high blood pressure is controlled by medication. Men level off at about 50 percent once they're past 70.

Younger women do have one concern that men of the same age don't share: high blood pressure during pregnancy. Actually, a woman's blood pressure usually drops during the first two trimesters of pregnancy, then rises during the final trimester. But if you develop high blood pressure during pregnancy, it can sometimes lead to complications such as a risky pregnancy or a low-birth-weight baby. That's why it's so important to have blood pressure readings taken at routine obstetric exams during pregnancy. We'll talk more about pregnancy and high blood pressure in chapter 6.

You probably noticed from the numbers above that younger African-Americans have a higher risk of developing hypertension than either whites or Mexican-Americans. Because African-Americans get high blood pressure earlier, its effects can be even greater. Compared with whites, African-Americans are 1.3 times more likely to have a non-fatal stroke, 1.8 times more likely to have a fatal stroke, 1.5 times more likely to die of heart diseases, and 5 times more likely to develop kidney failure.

The reasons for this increased risk aren't really known. Some doctors speculate that African-Americans, on the whole, are more sensitive to the effects of sodium. That is, too much salt in the diet affects them more than it does whites who eat the same amount. Other doctors believe that lifestyle differences—including poor diet, lack of exercise, and stress—play a role, too. Whatever the reason for the variation in risk, treatment for high blood pressure—including lifestyle changes and drug therapy—is equally effective in all races.

LOWERING THE NUMBERS

Being in a higher-risk group doesn't mean that you are automatically going to develop high blood pressure. You could be one of the lucky ones who avoids hypertension. And you can improve your luck by following many of the suggestions in this book, including which foods you eat and how much exercise you get.

Which brings us to the most important sentence in this whole book: *You can lower your blood pressure.*

The emphasis, you'll notice, is on you. While drugs can help lower blood pressure, they're not the first option. You can make changes in your lifestyle that may by themselves be enough to lower pressure naturally.

This probably means it's time to break some old habits. You can start by taking that saltshaker off the table. Pay attention to food labels, too, since sodium lurks in almost every canned or packaged food. But please don't think that changing your eating habits means never enjoying "good" food again. If you like canned salmon or macaroni and cheese, nobody is going to stop you from eating them once in a while. If you have always liked a glass of wine with dinner, go ahead and have one (but not much more).

If you like a piece of cheesecake now and again, that's okay, too. If you're eating the right foods most of the time, a little indulgence can feel good. In fact, it may keep you from going overboard later.

It's probably a good time to pry yourself off the sofa, too. You don't have to become a triathlete to lower blood pressure—but you do need to get some exercise. Start small, with a walk up the street. Eventually, you'll work your way up to 30 minutes or more, and you'll probably love the feeling. You can always tape that TV episode to watch when you get back.

How do you get started on this bold, new life? We'll lay everything out in detail in chapters 3 and 4.

Of course, sometimes lifestyle changes won't be enough. You may need to start taking high blood pressure medication, too. Blood pressure drugs have greatly improved over the years. While there may be side effects, they're usually minor. And there's such a wide variety of drugs now available—from diuretics to beta-blockers to ACE inhibitors and more—that you and your doctor should be able to find the medication and dose that will maximize benefits while keeping side effects to a minimum.

Still, your doctor can't help unless you're willing to help yourself. You'll need to do your part. Of the 50 million

Americans with hypertension, only half are getting the help they need—and less than half of them are doing everything it takes to make themselves healthy.

Hypertension is a serious disease, so don't fool around with it. It's vital that you get high blood pressure under control before it does damage to your body.

Now let's take a look at how doctors measure and classify high blood pressure.

CHAPTER 2

Off the Cuff:
The Keys to Diagnosis

As you can see by now, high blood pressure is serious business. But for all of the problems it can cause, you probably wouldn't even know you have it unless your doctor tells you so. You might get a few unexpected headaches. But other than that, hypertension has no symptoms in its early stages.

So it's not surprising that as many as 30 percent of people with high blood pressure are completely unaware that they have the problem. This means almost 15 million Americans could be getting treatment right now that could improve or even save their lives—but they're not. Many of them will not seek help until they've had hypertension for years and it starts to create other problems—chest pain, stroke, heart attack, heart failure, or kidney disease.

The good news is that it isn't hard to get checked for high blood pressure right now. Usually, it's as simple as sitting down, sticking out your arm, and waiting while a doctor or nurse runs a painless test. Let's take a few minutes to look at how this test works—and what all those numbers mean.

IT'S A WRAP

Hold out your left hand with your palm facing up. Place the index and middle fingers of your right hand gently across your left wrist, just below the thumb. Feel the blood pumping about once every second or so? That's your pulse. Every time your heart beats, it pushes fresh blood into your arteries and toward your body's hungry cells. With each heartbeat, your blood pressure goes up. And with each pause between beats, it drops a little. In other words, you really don't have a constant flow of blood, like water through a garden hose. It's more like an air pump that pushes bursts of air into a tire, pauses to create more pressure, then shoots in the air again.

A blood pressure reading measures both the pressure when the heart pumps and the pressure when it relaxes and reloads. The higher reading, when the heart pumps, is called systolic pressure. The lower reading, when the heart is at rest, is called diastolic pressure. These numbers are usually written with a slash between them, like 110/70 or 140/90. You'd read them as "110 over 70" or "140 over 90."

The most common device that measures blood pressure is called a sphygmomanometer. You've probably seen one in your doctor's office. It consists of an inflatable cuff, an air pump, and a gauge. The gauge may be electronic, may be a circular dial (termed *aneroid*), or it may be a column that looks like a giant thermometer. Like a thermometer, the column is filled with mercury. The higher the pressure goes, the higher the mercury rises in its tube.

Here's how the process works: Your doctor or nurse wraps the cuff snugly around your upper arm. She then places a stethoscope on the inside of your elbow. The stethoscope is a listening device that lets the person doing the measurement hear the pulse and blood flow in your arm. It's the same instrument that your doctor uses to listen to your lungs and heart.

HOW BLOOD PRESSURE IS MEASURED

Blood doesn't flow in an even stream. Instead, it moves in spurts, helped along by your heartbeat. When your heart pumps, your blood pressure rises. When it relaxes, your pressure drops. These two periods make up your blood pressure reading. Here's how doctors measure your blood pressure level:

A) An inflatable cuff is wrapped around your upper arm. Air is forced into the cuff until the cuff cuts off blood flow to your lower arm. Then, air is slowly released from the cuff.

B) The doctor or nurse uses a stethoscope to listen for a thumping sound. This comes at the exact time that blood starts flowing back into the lower arm. That level is the first measurement, called the systolic reading. In this case, the systolic reading is 120.

C) The doctor or nurse continues to let air out of the cuff. He or she listens for the point at which the thumping sound disappears. This level is called the diastolic reading. In this example, the diastolic reading is 80. That means the reading in this case is 120/80.

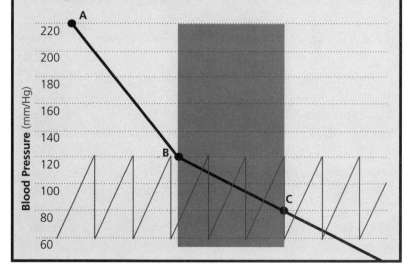

The cuff is slowly inflated. As it tightens around your arm, it starts to temporarily cut off the flow of blood to your lower arm. The tighter the cuff, the more restricted the blood flow. Finally, it stops altogether. This happens when the main artery in your arm, the brachial artery, gets squeezed so tightly that it collapses momentarily.

Now the readings begin. The doctor or nurse slowly releases the pressure in the cuff. Blood keeps trying to squeeze back through the brachial artery. Finally, the artery refills partway and shoots blood back into your lower arm. The person doing the measurement hears the rush of blood and a thumping sound through the stethoscope. She then looks at the pressure gauge and notices the level of mercury. The point at which blood pushes back through the artery is the systolic blood pressure reading. Remember, it's the higher of the two readings.

The traditional gauge is laid out in millimeters. So a reading of 130 means that your systolic blood pressure has pushed 130 millimeters of mercury up the column. It's written as 130 mm Hg, with *mm* standing for millimeter and *Hg* being the chemical symbol for mercury.

Okay, you're halfway done. The cuff keeps slowly deflating, and more and more blood flows through the brachial artery. But because there's still some air left in the cuff, the artery remains partially collapsed. The doctor or nurse can still hear the blood pumping. Eventually, the artery refills completely. That's when there's no more noise in the stethoscope. The doctor or nurse then checks the gauge again. The number she sees is the diastolic blood pressure reading. This shows what your blood pressure is when your heart is at rest between beats. Again, it's read in millimeters of mercury. So a typical diastolic reading might be 80 mm Hg.

There you have it: a blood pressure measurement of 130/80 mm Hg. Now let's take a look at what those numbers mean.

THE RESULTS ARE IN

The most nerve-racking part of taking any test is waiting for the results. This is where a blood pressure test is a lot more satisfying than your high school algebra exams—you get the results immediately. Here's what the numbers mean.

Optimal. If your systolic reading is 110 mm Hg or less and your diastolic reading is 70 mm Hg or less, congratulations! Your blood pressure is terrific. Your heart and blood vessels work together to push blood at just the right intensity to get the job done, without causing undue strain on your system.

Just remember that things can change over time. A good reading today doesn't mean that you can forget about high blood pressure forever. While blood pressure doesn't have to increase with age, it often does. Keep up your healthy habits and make sure you get rechecked for hypertension no later than two years from now.

Normal. If your systolic reading is between 110 and 129 mm Hg and your diastolic reading is between 70 and 84 mm Hg, you have normal blood pressure. This is pretty good, too, though not quite as desirable as the optimal level. Normal blood pressure means that your heart and blood vessels are getting the job done well, without causing too much strain. But there's still some room for improvement. Even at this level, damage can happen to your heart and blood vessels. You might want to think about eating a little bit better and getting a little more exercise—topics that we'll discuss in great detail later in the book.

MAKE YOUR READINGS COUNT

It's very important that your blood pressure be properly measured. Otherwise, you may end up with readings that are either too high or too low. You might think your blood pressure is high when it isn't—or, worse yet, think it's fine when you really have hypertension.

Here are a few rules that you should follow when getting your blood pressure checked.

1. Rest quietly for at least five minutes before the reading. Remember, your blood pressure rises when you are active. It takes a few minutes for your pressure to return to resting level—even if you've only been walking or you've climbed a few stairs to get to the doctor's office.

2. Don't drink anything with caffeine for at least 30 minutes before a measurement. Caffeine is a stimulant; it makes your whole body more active while it's in your system. That's great when you first wake up in the morning and need a little wake-up call. But it can lead to a blood pressure measurement that's too high, since caffeine often raises blood pressure temporarily.

3. Don't smoke for at least 30 minutes before a measurement. It's the same principle as drinking caffeine. The nicotine in a cigarette is a stimulant and can raise blood pressure for up to a half-hour after each smoke.

4. Make sure that you are seated upright and that both of your feet are placed flat on the floor. Believe it or not, blood pressure readings may be slightly different when you cross your legs or raise them off the floor.

5. Use the right-size cuff. Many adults have wide arms and need a larger cuff than usual. Most doctors will use a large cuff when they need to—but it can never hurt to remind them.

6. Hold your arm straight out, at heart level. It's best, in fact, if you sit at a table that supports your arm in this position. That way, you don't have to work as hard to hold out your arm. There's no need to keep your arm rigid, by the way. Just hold it straight enough that the doctor or nurse is able to wrap the cuff around your upper arm and place the stethoscope on the inside of your elbow.

7. Sit quietly while the doctor or nurse slowly deflates the cuff. This process should take at least 20 seconds. If the cuff deflates too fast, the mercury in the tube flows down too quickly to read with any accuracy.

8. Get at least two measurements at each sitting. Blood pressure can change quite a bit in a short amount of time. The average of two measurements is a better test of your blood pressure than any single measurement.

Doctors and nurses do a lot of blood pressure tests, and most of the time the results will be on target. Everyone makes mistakes, however. If you suspect that your blood pressure numbers aren't accurate—perhaps because they're dramatically different than they were in an earlier test—don't hesitate to ask that the test be repeated. Your doctor or nurse will be happy to oblige, and you'll rest easier knowing that the test correctly measured your blood pressure.

It's very important that you get an accurate reading. A change of as little as 5 to 10 mm Hg on the systolic or diastolic pressure can mean the difference between a high and a normal reading.

People with normal blood pressure levels should get rechecked within the next two years.

High-normal. If you have a systolic reading between 130 and 139 mm Hg or a diastolic reading between 85 and 89 mm Hg, your blood pressure is considered high-normal. Notice that we say "or," not "and." If either of your readings falls within either of these categories, your blood pressure is considered high-normal—no matter if the other reading is lower. For example, a measurement of 135/75 mm Hg is considered high-normal, even though the second reading (the diastolic reading) falls within the normal range.

Doctors don't consider people with high-normal readings to have hypertension. But things are getting too close for comfort. In fact, many people who fall into the high-normal range will start to develop problems related to high blood pressure, including the big ones: heart attack, stroke, and kidney disorders. A study of white Americans showed that men with readings of 120 to 139/80 mm Hg were 2.4 times more likely to die of heart disease than men with readings of less than 120/80 mm Hg. For white women with readings between 120 and 139/80 mm Hg, the risk was even higher: They were 4.8 times more likely to die of heart disease.

More than 30 million Americans fall within the high-normal blood pressure category. And more than half of them will eventually develop full-blown hypertension. So if your blood pressure is high-normal, consider this a wake-up call. It's certainly not too late to take control of the situation. A better diet and more exercise now could head off the need for medication later.

Stage 1 hypertension. If your systolic reading is between 140 and 159 mm Hg or your diastolic reading is between 90 and 99 mm Hg, you have Stage 1 hypertension. This used to be called mild hypertension, but doctors have stopped using that term. That's because there's nothing mild about any form of high blood pressure.

Scientific studies bear this out. One study of 145 men found that 7 percent of those with Stage 1 hypertension had left ventricular hypertrophy. No one with normal blood pressure readings had this condition. Doctors know that Stage 1 hypertension also leads to other heart-related problems and stroke. And a study of 5,500 men found that kidney function started to decline when diastolic blood pressure readings topped 95 mm Hg. The good news is that reducing diastolic readings below that level prevented further damage and sometimes even resulted in improvement of kidney function.

That's the key message for people with Stage 1 hypertension: It's not too late to make a difference. Your blood pressure has risen to the point where you're in danger of developing major health problems. But a combination of better diet, more exercise, and medication—done under your doctor's supervision—can push your readings back down to acceptable levels.

If your systolic and diastolic readings fall into different categories, the worse of the two readings dictates which category you fall into. For example, a reading of 140/80 mm Hg is considered Stage 1 hypertension, even though the diastolic reading (80 mm Hg) falls within the normal range.

One high reading isn't enough to confirm that you have Stage 1 hypertension. Your blood pressure level changes throughout the day, depending on whether you're exercising, drinking coffee, sleeping, or working. Your doctor will want to check your pressure at least three times to make sure that your resting blood pressure is truly high. The more readings you take, the more likely you are to get an accurate picture of things.

Stage 2 hypertension. People with systolic readings of 160 to 179 mm Hg or diastolic readings of 100 to 109 mm Hg have Stage 2 hypertension. This used to be called moderate hypertension. But again, there's nothing moderate about it, since it puts you at much higher risk of developing serious health problems.

One international report shows how dangerous Stage 2 hypertension can be when it comes to stroke. The survey followed nearly 13,000 men over the course of 25 years. That's a long time, during which people naturally die of a variety of causes, from accidents to heart attacks. Among men with systolic readings of 125 mm Hg or less (considered normal), 3.2 percent of those who died had suffered strokes. But among those with systolic readings topping 160 mm Hg (Stage 2 hypertension), the rate jumped to 13.8 percent.

As with Stage 1 hypertension, people who have readings that fall within the Stage 2 range need to get several more readings to confirm their blood pressure. Treatment with medication, along with improved diet and more exercise, should begin soon after diagnosis.

Stage 3 hypertension. A systolic reading of 180 or higher or a diastolic reading of 110 or higher indicates Stage 3 hypertension. This is an extremely serious condition. People with readings like these are in danger of developing heart, kidney, or eye damage or having a stroke. Your doctor will immediately retest your blood pressure, then start you on medication—often in the same visit. The sooner you get things under control, the better your chances of avoiding harm.

Isolated systolic hypertension. This type of high blood pressure occurs when the systolic reading is higher than normal but the diastolic reading remains in the optimal to high-normal range. Isolated systolic hypertension, or ISH, typically affects older people. Nearly two in three Americans aged 65 and older develop ISH. Doctors have long known that ISH can increase the risk of cardiovascular diseases. But until recently, there was some debate as to whether treating the problem helped lower the risk. That changed when doctors looked at results from the Systolic Hypertension in the Elderly Program.

This nationwide study looked at 4,736 men and women who had ISH, with systolic readings exceeding 160 mm Hg. Researchers treated half of the group with medication to lower blood pressure and gave the other half placebos—pills without medication. The researchers found that those who received medication had an overall lower death rate than those who got placebos. Specifically, those taking medication experienced 36 percent fewer strokes and 27 percent fewer heart attacks. They also developed fewer cases of congestive heart failure.

Doctors also believe that ISH can cause a condition called carotid artery stenosis. This is a narrowing of the carotid artery, which carries blood to the head and brain. Stenosis occurs when plaque forms in the artery and sticks to the walls, restricting the flow of blood. The researchers conducting the senior citizen study found that stenosis got worse in 31 percent of those taking placebos compared with just 14 percent of those who were taking real medication.

Thanks to this study, doctors now recommend that people with ISH get treatment. For people with systolic readings over 160 mm Hg, medication should be started. For those with systolic readings between 140 and 160 mm

Hg, a better diet and more exercise may be enough. If not, medication will be needed.

Malignant hypertension. This is the most serious high blood pressure condition of all. When people develop malignant hypertension, their blood pressure readings soar —typically to levels as high as over 130 mm Hg diastolic. About 1 in every 100 people with hypertension has malignant hypertension, and it's most common in those about 40 years of age. It often occurs when a person who is already on medication for high blood pressure abruptly stops taking it.

Malignant hypertension can be fatal if it's not immediately treated. Without treatment, most people will die within six months to one year. The condition can cause a host of problems in the central nervous system, including seizures, blurred vision (possibly even blindness), powerful headaches, drowsiness, and loss of consciousness. Together, these symptoms are called hypertensive encephalopathy.

The extremely high blood pressure levels in malignant hypertension can also cause hemorrhagic stroke, burst blood vessels, heart attack, and congestive heart failure. In short, if you are diagnosed with malignant hypertension, do exactly what your doctor says. Immediately. Your life depends on it.

HOME MEASUREMENTS

As we've seen, your blood pressure constantly changes. It dips when you're sleeping at night and shoots up when you're active, frightened, or under stress. People often get a little nervous when they go to their doctors for heart problems or even routine checkups. As you would expect, this can also cause your blood pressure to rise. The result is a bit of a Catch-22. The one time you need your blood pressure to be "accurate" is the time it's likely to be higher than usual. Doctors have a term for this type of "false high" reading: white coat hypertension. Some studies show that white coat hypertension can have a powerful effect on blood pressure readings. As many as 20 percent of people who have readings that fall in the Stage 1 category may not really have high blood pressure at all. They may just be nervous, and the higher reading reflects this.

If you feel that stress and anxiety are causing your blood pressure to be artificially high, don't hesitate to mention this to your doctor. He may decide that the only way to get an accurate reading is for you to take your own blood pressure at home, using a home monitoring device.

Before we talk about these home devices, we need to mention that white coat hypertension isn't always a "false high" reading. In fact, one study has found that people with this condition are more likely to have left ventricular hypertrophy and stiffened blood vessels than people whose readings in the doctor's office are normal. The topic is controversial, but some researchers believe that white coat hypertension may be the first step toward full-blown high blood pressure. There aren't enough studies to say for sure, but it may be that people with this condition could benefit from immediate drug treatment for high blood pressure, even though their readings at home appear normal.

In many cases, however, your doctor will decide to delay treatment until he has a chance to see what your blood pressure is at home, when you're in a comfortable, familiar place. Even if you're already being treated for high blood pressure, home monitoring may be a helpful way to track how medication or lifestyle changes are working. To measure your blood pressure at home, you'll need some equipment: an inflatable cuff, a gauge, and sometimes a stethoscope. All cuffs are basically made the same. They have a rubber bladder inside that fills with air and squeezes your arm. Most have a nylon outer layer and a Velcro fastener to hold the cuff in place. The easiest ones to use have an attached metal loop that allows you to pull it tight. Be sure to buy the right-size cuff. Adults with average-size arms should buy the regular size. If you have a large arm, make sure you buy a large cuff. Otherwise, your readings will probably be too high.

You'll have several choices of gauges, which are also called sphygmomanometers. The one that will give you the most accurate readings is the mercury column gauge. But it has one big drawback: It's filled with a harmful liquid. So it's probably best to avoid this kind—especially if you have children around the house. The second type is called an aneroid sphygmomanometer, which uses metal springs to measure changes in pressure. It's probably your best choice. The third type is electronic, which often is more expensive and sometimes less accurate.

Blood pressure machines are often sold in kits and can range in price from $40 to more than $100. There are dozens of kits on the market. Unfortunately, not all of them are accurate or easy to use, so before you purchase a kit, make sure that you can return it. And don't buy a cuff designed for your finger, because this type isn't accurate.

After you carefully read the instructions, try to get a reading. Then take the device with you to your next doctor's appointment. Let your doctor watch you get a reading to make sure that you're doing it the right way and that the machine is accurate.

Taking your own blood pressure is a bit tricky, especially at first. (One solution is to have a family member or friend help you.) The procedure is the same as in your doctor's office. Sit in a comfortable chair with an armrest or at a table, so you can hold your arm in a position that's just about as high as your heart. Rest for at least 5 minutes before taking a measurement. Make sure you haven't had any caffeine or smoked a cigarette for at least 30 minutes before beginning.

Put the cuff over your bare upper arm, making sure the cuff fits snugly but not too tightly. You should be able to slip two fingers underneath the cuff, but not much more. Fasten the cuff with the Velcro closure. The tubing on the cuff should be placed on the inside of your elbow, just above the main artery. Putting on your own cuff takes a little practice, but you'll quickly get the hang of it.

Place the middle and index fingers of your "free" hand over the inside of the opposite elbow, just below the cuff. Find the pulse in your artery. Then place the head of the stethoscope (also called the *bell*) over the spot. Straighten out your arm.

It's time to inflate the cuff. Squeeze the bulb quickly, so the cuff blows up rapidly. Stop when the pressure on the gauge reads 30 mm Hg more than your typical systolic reading.

Now let the cuff deflate very slowly. The whole process should take at least 20 seconds. Listen with the stethoscope. You shouldn't hear anything at first, since the brachial artery is collapsed and no blood is flowing. Keep watching the gauge and listening for a thumping sound.

When you hear the thump, note where the needle on the gauge is pointing. That's your systolic pressure.

Continue deflating the cuff very slowly. You will still hear sounds in the stethoscope, as the artery slowly opens and more and more blood flows into the lower arm. What you're listening for now is the point at which the noises stop. When you can no longer hear anything in the stethoscope, note the reading on the gauge. That's your diastolic pressure.

Make sure that you take at least two readings every time. Wait two minutes or more between the readings, so your blood pressure stays at your typical level. Most readings are within 5 mm Hg of each other for both the systolic and diastolic measurements. If not, take a third reading. Then average the measurements. If your systolic readings are 150, 160, and 155, the average would be 155 (150 + 160 + 155 = 465; 465 ÷ 3 = 155). If your diastolic readings are 90, 100, and 90, the average would be 93 (90 + 100 + 90 = 280; 280 ÷ 3 = 93.33).

Always make sure you use the same arm each time you take a measurement. And it's a good idea to do the readings at about the same time each day, so you get measurements that you can compare with each other. Remember, your blood pressure changes throughout the day. If you take it right after you wake up one day and right after lunch the next day, you cannot compare the results.

By the way, the gauges on your blood pressure monitor will lose their accuracy over time. So it's a good idea to get them checked at least once a year. When you buy the device, ask the salesperson if she'll adjust it for free.

If you can manage to work with it, the cuff-and-stethoscope system will give you the most consistent readings.

BLOOD PRESSURE TO GO

Home monitoring isn't the answer for everyone. In some cases, your doctor may ask you to wear what's called an ambulatory device. This has a cuff that goes around your arm and a monitor that fits on your belt. It measures your pressure automatically during the day, usually every 15-20 minutes. You wear it for a full day—even when you sleep—and it keeps a log of your readings at various times. You'll probably be asked to keep a journal of what you were doing each time the cuff inflated.

The ambulatory device can give your doctor a precise picture of how your blood pressure rises and falls during the day and night. This has a couple of advantages. First, it may help identify people with white coat hypertension, especially those who can't use home monitors. Since the readings come at random times, you won't get all worked up about somebody checking your blood pressure. In some cases, people with high readings in the doctor's office turn out to have optimal or normal blood pressure when it gets checked with ambulatory devices.

Second, the automatic monitor can check how your blood pressure medication is working. This is sometimes done for people who have high readings despite taking several medications. Sometimes a monitor shows that you're actually doing quite well with your medicine, even though blood pressure readings in the doctor's office may be higher than what's expected.

Usually, the ambulatory monitor is a onetime procedure. Your doctor will ask you to wear it for 24 or 48 hours, and then you're done. You won't need to use it again unless your doctor wants to check up on your medication later on.

But if things don't work out and there's no one who can take the readings for you, you may still want to consider a top-quality electronic machine. They have gotten better over the years, and some of them can give you reliable measurements. For a summary of electronic home blood pressure monitors, see Appendix 2 on page 179.

DON'T WASTE YOUR CHANGE

How about those coin-operated blood pressure machines you see in malls and pharmacies? Well, they really aren't very accurate. First of all, you've probably done some walking—either around the mall or from your car—before you sit down at the machine. Most people don't have the discipline or the time to wait for five minutes before getting readings. You also have to remember to take off your jacket and roll up your sleeve, so the cuff inflates around your bare arm. And even if you wait for five minutes and roll up your sleeve, there's still a good chance you won't get a proper reading. That's because many of these machines are not calibrated. They may never have been checked for accuracy, so there's no telling what your true reading is.

Sometimes you'll run across a free blood pressure screening—maybe at church, the mall, or a senior center. The people who take your readings at these clinics usually have proper equipment. And they usually have good training. But they still have to follow the same rules your doctor does. That means letting you rest for at least five minutes, making sure you keep your feet on the floor, elevating your arm to heart level, releasing air from the cuff very slowly, and so on.

An Important Warning

Home monitoring devices provide an important service by allowing people to get accurate blood pressure readings at home. But home monitoring is not a substitute for a doctor's care. Even if you don't have hypertension, you need to get your blood pressure checked by a doctor or nurse at least once every two years. If you do have high blood pressure, don't use your home readings as an excuse to change diet or medication—or to cancel your doctor's appointment. If your blood pressure drops to optimal, that's great. But always check with your doctor before you change anything. Stopping or changing medication by yourself can be extremely dangerous.

The Next Step

When your systolic reading reaches 140 mm Hg or your diastolic reading reaches 90 mm Hg on a regular basis, it's time to face facts. You have hypertension. It's certainly not the end of the world, because in most cases, you can do something to bring your reading back to optimal or at least closer to optimal. In fact, you should consider yourself lucky that you're finding out about it now instead of years from now. You can save your body a lot of damage by taking action immediately.

Unless you have an extremely high reading, your doctor will probably take a little bit of time to sort things out before prescribing any medication. The first thing he's likely to do is to see if there are any obvious causes for your high blood pressure.

Remember, in 95 percent or more of all hypertension cases, doctors don't know exactly what is causing it. They call this primary hypertension. It probably results from some combination of consuming too much salt, drinking too much alcohol, weighing too much, adopting bad eating habits, not exercising enough, and having the wrong genes. Your doctor can make some educated guesses about what's causing your blood pressure to rise, but he won't be able to tell you for sure.

But in the remaining 5 percent of cases, there's an underlying reason for high readings. It could be something as simple as a reaction to medication, either prescription or over-the-counter. It could be a hormone imbalance caused by a growth on one of your adrenal glands or some other problem. It could be a problem with your kidneys or even a narrowed aorta.

To find out what's going on, your doctor is going to ask you lots of questions about your medical history. Here's a sample of what he'll want to know.

+ Do you drink alcohol? If so, how much and how often?
+ Are you taking any prescription or over-the-counter drugs?
+ Do you have diabetes?
+ Do you smoke?
+ Does anyone in your family have high blood pressure?
+ How much salt do you eat?
+ How is your overall diet? Is it high in saturated fat or cholesterol?
+ Has your weight changed greatly over the years?
+ Are you under lots of stress at work or at home?

Your doctor will also want to know if you have any symptoms of kidney or adrenal gland problems. For example, headaches, excessive sweating, and a pounding heartbeat can be signs of a tumor on one of the adrenal glands.

You'll probably need a complete physical exam, too, which will allow your doctor to identify what problems, if any, your blood pressure has already caused. In addition to the usual height and weight measurements, you can also expect the following:

- An eye exam to make sure that there's no damage to your retinas.
- A heart checkup to be certain that it beats at a regular pace and rhythm. Your doctor will also listen for a heart murmur or other unusual sounds. You may need a chest X-ray to see if your heart is a normal size.
- An examination of your pulse at various points on your body. Your doctor will check the carotid arteries in your neck to make sure there is no murmur or another sign that they've narrowed. He'll also check your abdomen to see if there is a murmur or an aneurysm in your aorta.
- A check for symptoms of congestive heart failure. For example, your doctor will look for swelling in your legs and listen for fluid in your lungs, which can be signs that your heart isn't able to pump blood very efficiently.
- More blood pressure readings. In some cases, your doctor will measure your blood pressure while you are standing and sitting. This is to make sure that you aren't prone to a sudden drop in blood pressure when you stand up. This condition is called orthostatic hypotension. It can make you feel light-headed or dizzy and could cause you to lose your balance.

You might also get your blood pressure checked at your ankles. It should be about the same reading as in your arms. But if the ankle readings are much lower than the arm readings, you might have narrowing of the arteries in your legs. This is called peripheral artery disease. People with this condition are at significantly greater risk for heart attack and other heart problems.

Your doctor may also order a neurological examination to see if you've had a stroke. He'll want to know, too, if you're experiencing severe stress or other problems.

If your doctor is concerned that you may have already suffered some heart or kidney damage, additional tests may be necessary. Here's a partial list of the tests you might expect.

- Urinalysis, to check for blood and protein in the urine.
- Cholesterol count, including total cholesterol, triglycerides, "bad" LDL, and "good" HDL cholesterol. High total cholesterol and high LDL cholesterol levels are risk factors for heart disease.
- Electrocardiogram (ECG), to check the heart for conditions such as left ventricular hypertrophy.
- Blood tests for sodium, potassium, calcium, protein, glucose, creatinine, and uric acid. Low levels of potassium could indicate adrenal gland problems. High levels of glucose could indicate diabetes, which is a risk factor for heart disease. High levels of creatinine and uric acid could mean kidney trouble.

Not everyone will get all of these tests. Based on your medical history and the physical exam, your doctor may determine that you simply have primary hypertension. If that's the case, you probably won't need to spend time or money getting a complete lab workup. But if you don't respond well to treatment or your readings rise dramatically over a short period of time, it could mean you have an underlying health problem that's causing secondary hypertension. Additional tests will be necessary.

Now you have a better understanding of what high blood pressure can do—and a better idea of how you and your doctor can tell if you have hypertension. In the next chapter, we'll talk about treating it. It will take some combination of dietary changes, exercise, and, in many cases, medication. But the results will certainly be worth the effort.

CHAPTER 3

How to Lower the Numbers

High blood pressure almost never appears overnight. Most cases take years and years to develop, helped along by factors such as an improper diet and lack of exercise.

So if you've just found out that you have hypertension, don't be surprised if your doctor takes some time to treat it before giving you medication. Unless you have Stage 2 hypertension or higher, your doctor will probably recommend that you start your treatment by making some basic lifestyle changes. This doesn't apply if you have another health problem such as kidney failure or heart disease, or another risk factor for heart disease—particularly diabetes. If you have any of these problems, you'll probably get medication right off the bat.

Usually, it's a step-by-step process. You start by making changes in your lifestyle. If they're enough to lower your blood pressure, terrific! There won't be a second or third step. If you need a little more help to control hypertension, your doctor will begin treating you with medication—but only enough to do the job. If you need additional help, your doctor may switch medications in search of one that

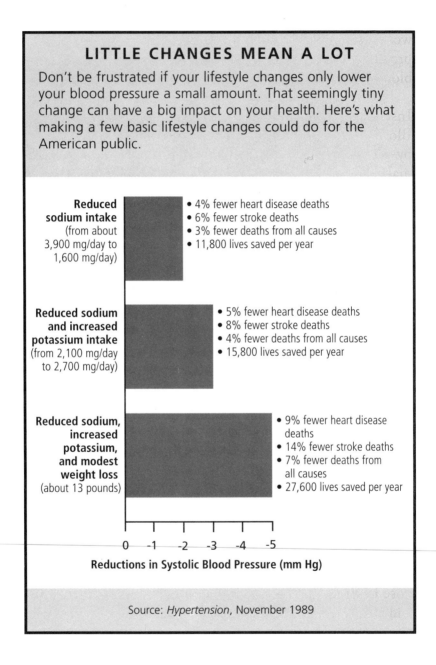

LITTLE CHANGES MEAN A LOT

Don't be frustrated if your lifestyle changes only lower your blood pressure a small amount. That seemingly tiny change can have a big impact on your health. Here's what making a few basic lifestyle changes could do for the American public.

Reduced sodium intake (from about 3,900 mg/day to 1,600 mg/day)

- 4% fewer heart disease deaths
- 6% fewer stroke deaths
- 3% fewer deaths from all causes
- 11,800 lives saved per year

Reduced sodium and increased potassium intake (from 2,100 mg/day to 2,700 mg/day)

- 5% fewer heart disease deaths
- 8% fewer stroke deaths
- 4% fewer deaths from all causes
- 15,800 lives saved per year

Reduced sodium, increased potassium, and modest weight loss (about 13 pounds)

- 9% fewer heart disease deaths
- 14% fewer stroke deaths
- 7% fewer deaths from all causes
- 27,600 lives saved per year

0 -1 -2 -3 -4 -5

Reductions in Systolic Blood Pressure (mm Hg)

Source: *Hypertension*, November 1989

works better for you. If that still doesn't do it, she may prescribe two or more medicines at once to bring your blood pressure down.

Experts from around the country and from the National Institutes of Health and the National Heart, Lung, and Blood Institute have worked together to develop a step-by-step approach to treating hypertension. It's designed to make sure you get enough treatment, but not too much. There's no sense in taking more medication than is absolutely necessary—especially since most medications will cause at least some side effects. Here's the step-by-step plan they recommend for bringing blood pressure down.

Step 1: Lifestyle changes. There are six biggies here: losing weight, exercising regularly, reducing salt intake, moderating alcohol consumption, improving diet, and quitting smoking. Not all of these apply in every case, of course. If you don't smoke, that's great. And if you don't drink, this is not the time to start.

In many cases, these lifestyle changes will be enough to drop your blood pressure to a safe level. Even if they don't, they're still very important for your overall health. Better nutrition and more exercise will strengthen your body and help fight heart disease and other illnesses down the road.

Step 2: Lifestyle changes plus medication. It's not unusual to need a little more help than lifestyle changes alone. If your blood pressure doesn't drop to a safe level by making the basic changes in Step 1, you're probably going to need some medication. The drugs usually used at this stage are either beta-blockers or diuretics, in the lowest dose possible. Both types of drugs have been proven safe and effective over decades of use.

Step 3: Increased medication. If the first class of drugs doesn't do the trick, don't despair. Your doctor has other medications at her disposal. In Step 3, you'll try a higher dose of a beta-blocker or diuretic. Or you may switch from one of those drugs to the other. Or you may be given another drug, such as an ACE (angiotensin converting enzyme) inhibitor or a calcium channel blocker. Of course, you won't stop with the lifestyle changes; they'll be a part of your everyday life from now on.

Step 4: Multiple medications. If your high blood pressure turns out to be very stubborn, you may need to take several medications at once. Again, there are dozens of drugs available, so the odds are good that your doctor will find just the right combination for you. It's all a matter of fine-tuning your treatment plan.

We'll talk more about drugs in chapter 5. But for now, let's take a closer look at lifestyle changes, since they're really the cornerstone of controlling most cases of high blood pressure. We'll start by looking at the foods you eat—and how you can make them work for you in the battle against high blood pressure.

THE POWER OF DIET

Let's get the D-word—diet—out of the way right now. Like it or not, lowering your blood pressure is going to mean changing the way you eat. This doesn't mean you're doomed to a life of rice cakes, nonfat plain yogurt, and wheat germ (although eating these things once in a while certainly won't hurt). You're just going to have to eat more of some foods, such as fruits, vegetables, whole grains, and beans. And you'll have to cut back on other foods, such as red meat, potato chips, and alcohol. These can hurt your chances of beating hypertension.

There are two major reasons for changing your diet. First, it will help you lose weight. This is extremely important in the battle against high blood pressure. Forty percent of all people with hypertension are obese. Fortunately, you don't have to lose a lot of weight to make a significant improvement in your blood pressure. Losing as few as 10 pounds can drop your systolic pressure by about 7 mm Hg. This alone can mean the difference between Stage 1 hypertension and high-normal blood pressure. In fact, one in every four people with high blood pressure is able to control it just by losing weight.

If you don't have high blood pressure, shedding a few extra pounds may help keep your blood pressure in the normal or optimal range. Several scientific studies have documented this benefit from weight loss. Researchers have found that people with high-normal blood pressure (between 130 and 139 mm Hg systolic or 85 and 89 mm Hg diastolic) who lost six to nine pounds had reductions of 1.3 to 2.9 mm Hg in systolic pressure and 1.2 to 2.3 mm Hg in diastolic pressure. That's not a whole lot, but it paid off in the long run. Over the next three to five years, people who dropped the pounds were much less likely to develop full-blown hypertension than those who didn't.

The second reason for changing your diet is more basic. Doctors now believe that the foods you eat affect your blood pressure, regardless of whether you lose weight. High-salt diets can hurt. High-fat diets can hurt. Low-potassium diets can hurt. But diets rich in fruits, vegetables, and low-fat dairy foods can work magic against hypertension.

How do you get started? Well, first let's see if you need to lose weight.

Optimal Weights for Men and Women
(in pounds)

Height (in shoes)	Small Frame	Medium Frame	Large Frame
Men			
5'6"	124-133	130-143	138-156
5'7"	128-137	134-147	142-161
5'8"	132-141	138-152	147-166
5'9"	136-145	142-156	151-170
5'10"	140-150	146-160	155-174
5'11"	144-154	150-165	159-179
6'0"	148-158	154-170	164-184
6'1"	152-162	158-175	168-189
6'2"	156-167	162-180	173-194
Women			
5'1"	99-107	104-116	112-128
5'2"	102-110	107-119	115-131
5'3"	105-113	110-122	118-134
5'4"	108-116	113-126	121-138
5'5"	111-119	116-130	125-142
5'6"	114-123	120-135	129-146
5'7"	118-127	124-139	133-150
5'8"	122-131	128-143	137-154
5'9"	126-135	132-147	141-158

(Source: Metropolitan Life Insurance Company)

Don't be shocked if you're over your optimal weight. Millions of Americans are. And your goal needn't be to achieve model thinness, since losing just a few pounds can have substantial medical benefits. Try to lose weight gradually. It can take months, maybe even a year or two, to bring yourself back to a healthy weight.

If you are seriously overweight, don't go it alone. Ask your doctor to help plan a safe and effective strategy for losing weight. And by all means avoid crash and fad diets. They are dangerous. Repeat: They are dangerous. All-grapefruit diets and no-protein diets and Hollywood-celebrity diets can throw your body way out of balance. Using diuretics without your doctor's approval can create mineral imbalances that can be extremely dangerous. And diet pills often contain stimulants that can actually raise blood pressure or cause heart problems.

Most doctors recommend following a diet that will enable you to lose a pound or two a week. Within six months, you can lose close to 25 pounds. Considering that it can take years to become heavy, that's hardly too long to wait to become thinner and healthier.

The secret to losing weight is to burn more calories. Calories come from two sources: the foods you eat and the energy your body stores. When you eat less, your body is forced to use its energy stores—namely, fat—to make up the difference in calories.

There are two ways to accelerate the fat-burning process. The first is through exercise. If you make your body work harder—on the treadmill, by lifting weights, or even by walking a few flights of stairs—you'll burn more calories. We're going to talk about exercise in more detail in chapter 4.

The second way is to eat fewer calories. Again, when your body doesn't have as many calories from food to burn, it will need to tap its fat stores. How many calories do you need? That's the $64,000 question. Everyone burns calories at a different rate, so it's impossible to be exact. But as a general rule, you need to eat about 12 calories per pound of body weight each day to maintain your present weight—and a little less than that to lose weight. This figure is higher for younger folks and men, lower for older people and women.

TYPICAL DAILY CALORIE REQUIREMENTS

Weight (lbs.)	Daily Calories (to maintain weight)
100	1,200
110	1,320
120	1,440
130	1,560
140	1,680
150	1,800
160	1,920
170	2,040
180	2,160
190	2,280
200	2,400

Let's say your ideal weight is 140 pounds. According to the chart, you need to eat about 1,680 calories a day—a little more if you're fairly active. If you're over your ideal weight, you're almost surely eating more than that right now.

How can you tell how many calories you're eating? Read labels! Every packaged food now indicates how many calories a serving contains. A can of soup, for instance, may contain 300 calories per serving. Note the words "per serving." One can of soup may have three servings—which means eating the whole can gives you 900 calories, not 300. We don't eat only packaged foods, of course. This means calorie counts aren't always available. To help you keep track, here's a list of some common foods and the calories they contain in a typical serving.

CALORIES IN COMMON FOODS

Food	Calories per Serving
Fruits	
Apple, medium	80
Banana, medium	105
Blueberries, 1 cup	80
Cantaloupe, 1 cup	55
Dates, 5 medium	115
Figs, 3 dried	145
Grapefruit, ½ medium	40
Grapes, 1 cup	60
Nectarine, medium	70
Orange, medium	60
Peach, medium	40
Pear, medium	100
Pineapple, 1 cup	75
Raisins, ½ cup	220
Strawberries, 1 cup	45

Food	Calories per Serving
Vegetables	
Asparagus, ½ cup cooked	25
Broccoli, ½ cup cooked	20
Carrot, 1 raw, medium	30
Corn, 1 ear	85
Lettuce, romaine, 1 cup	10
Onion, ½ cup cooked	30
Pepper, green, ½ cup	15
Potato, baked, medium	220
Spinach, ½ cup cooked	20
Squash, acorn, ½ cup	60
Sweet potato, medium	120
Tomato, medium	25
Meats, Poultry, and Fish*	
Meats:	
Brisket	210
Filet mignon	180
Ground beef (extra lean)	220
Ham, fresh	190
Lamb, leg	160
Pot roast	185
Steak, T-bone	180
Poultry:	
Chicken, breast	140
Turkey, breast	135

Food	Calories per Serving
Fish:	
Cod	90
Flounder	100
Halibut	120
Mackerel	225
Salmon, Chinook	100

*Calories based on 3 ounces of lean meat, poultry, or fish, broiled or roasted.

Losing weight isn't about counting calories down to the last crumb of bread, however. There are lots of important things that calories don't tell you, like how much salt or fat is in a food. But sometimes keeping track of what you eat can be a real eye-opener. So try it for a few days. Keep a list of everything you eat, and estimate the number of calories you consume. This should give you some idea of how much extra energy you're taking in every day. Remember: Every extra calorie gets stored in your body as fat. And fat is just what you're trying to get rid of.

Once you figure out about how many calories you're eating per day, try cutting the total by about 500. This alone will result in you losing about one pound per week!

TIME FOR A SHAKEDOWN

Quick—name the one thing that most Americans eat 25 times too much of. Fat? Sugar? Cholesterol?

Guess again. It's sodium. You get it from canned foods. You get it from meat. You get it from cheese, cereal, soup, pretzels, chips, tuna, bread, spaghetti sauce, and hundreds of other foods. Every day, the average American adult eats between 3,500 and 5,000 milligrams of sodium—way, way more than the 200 or so milligrams we need to survive. Where does all of this sodium come from? Salt—which is also known as sodium chloride. Every grain of salt is about 40 percent sodium.

We talked earlier about how sodium affects blood pressure. Essentially, it causes your kidneys to retain water in your body. The more water you retain, the more fluid you have in your bloodstream. This means your heart has to pump harder, which can cause higher blood pressure. Sodium can also cause small blood vessels to constrict, making your heart work even harder to squeeze blood through the smaller openings.

So why do we eat so much more sodium than we need to? Well, in all honesty, it tastes good. Many of us grew up salting everything from steak to eggs. It's a habit. Lots of people can't look at a baked potato without shaking salt on it first.

Still, the saltshaker is just a small part of the problem. We get only about 15 percent of our salt by adding it at the dinner table. As much as 70 percent of the salt we eat every day comes from processed foods. Almost all canned and packaged foods contain sodium—often a lot of it. A single can of soup, for instance, may contain 1,000 milligrams of sodium, enough to cover your body's needs for five days. Condiments such as ketchup are virtual sodium bombs. Even sweet-tasting foods such as breakfast cereals and sweet rolls can be packed with salt.

With all this salt in the supermarket, how can you avoid the stuff? Here are a few tips:

Choose plenty of produce. Don't race through the produce aisle on your way to the Twinkies. Fresh and frozen fruits and vegetables are naturally low in sodium. One-half of a grapefruit, for example, has exactly zero milligrams of sodium, and a banana has one milligram. In fact, it's hard to find any fruit or vegetable with a significant amount of sodium—unless it is in a can and has added salt.

Skip the salt. This might sound radical, but take that saltshaker off your table. Put it in a drawer. Use it as a paperweight. With all of the sodium lurking in processed foods, there's no need whatsoever to add to the problem.

If you have a powerful "salt tooth," don't give up salting all at once. Try cutting back a little bit at a time. Use one shake instead of two, and don't automatically salt anything. Before you reach for the shaker, take a couple of bites. You can always add a little salt later, and you may find that your taste buds don't really need as much salt as you've been using.

Savor the flavor. Salt isn't the only taste that can tempt your tongue. Try experimenting with different herbs and spices when you cook. A little bit of fresh basil tastes great on a tomato. Maybe you'll like oregano on your lima beans or hot pepper on your chicken. Just play around until you find things you like. Soon you probably won't miss the salt at all. (In fact, many studies have shown that people get accustomed to the taste of low-salt foods.) And since 15 percent of all of the salt we eat gets added during cooking or at the table, it's a great place to start cutting back.

Start reading labels. The government now requires that all packaged foods have detailed nutrition labels. Next time you grab a can of tuna, turn it around and take a look. The label will tell you exactly how much sodium a serving contains. Remember that cans and boxes of food usually contain more than one serving. That tuna may have 350 milligrams of sodium per serving, but the can may contain three servings. So if you eat the whole can, you have to multiply 350 by 3 to get the total amount of sodium. That's 1,050 milligrams!

Also look for hidden salt. Most people don't realize that breads and cereals provide almost one-third of all of the salt we eat.

Know the lingo. Food packages can be a little sneaky sometimes. Just because a salsa jar says "reduced sodium" doesn't mean the salsa is low in sodium. It just means the salsa has less sodium than the regular version. A label that says "low-sodium" is a better bet. "Low-sodium" means the product has no more than 140 milligrams of sodium per serving.

Know your limits. Doctors recommend that you eat no more than 2,400 milligrams of sodium per day. It's not your goal to reach 2,400 milligrams per day. It's your goal to eat as little of that amount as possible.

Researchers have found that cutting daily sodium intake to 2,400 milligrams can really help people with hypertension. If you have high blood pressure, reducing your sodium consumption to this level can lower your systolic reading by 5 to 10 mm Hg and your diastolic readings by 2 to 5 mm Hg. If you have Stage 1 hypertension, this by itself can be enough to bring your readings back to normal levels. In fact, achieving normal blood pressure can happen in nearly 50 percent of all cases. Imagine: Cutting back on salt might be enough to keep you off blood pressure medication. It's certainly worth a try.

Most people are sensitive to the effects of salt to some degree. But some groups of people are likely to be more sensitive than others. Older people, African-Americans, those with very high blood pressure, and those with family histories of hypertension will see their blood pressure drop the most when they limit their salt intake.

Reducing salt consumption should be healthful for most people. But in a few cases, it can be dangerous. This is sometimes true for people with certain kidney diseases, who might have trouble keeping enough sodium in their systems. And people who tend to faint a lot might make things worse by reducing the amount of salt they eat. If you have one of these problems, talk to your doctor before cutting back too much on salt.

PILE ON THE POTASSIUM

When most people start trying to eat better, they think of all of the "nos" in their new diets. No salt. No fat. No fun. Well, there's one nutrient you can say yes to in a big way: potassium.

Doctors have found that blood pressure levels tend to be highest in countries where potassium intake is lowest. That includes America, where processed foods rob our diets of potassium. It's an important nutrient—one that affects how your heart, nervous system, and muscles function.

Just how potassium affects blood pressure isn't known for sure, but the connection seems strong. More than 30 studies have shown that taking potassium supplements reduces blood pressure in people with normal or high readings. You should only take them if they are prescribed by your doctor, however. Research has also shown that increasing the amount of potassium in the diet can help lower blood pressure in people who already have hypertension.

One study looked at 54 people who were taking medicine to control their blood pressure. Their average readings at the beginning of the study were 160 mm Hg systolic and

95 mm Hg diastolic—still high even though they were on medication. Half of the people in the study switched to a high-potassium diet for one year, while the other half continued with their usual diets. At the end of the year, 81 percent of those who started eating more potassium were able to cut their medication in half. That was much better than the people on their regular diet, only 29 percent of whom were able to cut back on their doses.

African-American people may especially benefit from increasing their intake of potassium. The diets of many African-Americans are very low in potassium to begin with. In one study, African-Americans who took potassium supplements saw drops in their blood pressure readings of 7 mm Hg systolic and 2.5 mm Hg diastolic over the course of three weeks.

As with every nutrient, it's better to get your potassium the old-fashioned way—in your diet. Fortunately, it's easy to do. Lots of foods are high in potassium. Here's a list.

POTASSIUM-RICH FOODS

Food	Milligrams per Serving
Apricots, 3 medium	313
Asparagus, boiled, ½ cup	144
Avocado, 1 medium	1,484
Banana, 1 medium	451
Black-eyed peas, boiled, 1 cup	689
Broccoli, boiled, ½ cup	228
Cantaloupe, 1 cup	494
Carrot, 1 medium	233
Dates, dried, 10	541

Food	Milligrams per Serving
Grapefruit, ½	175
Green beans, boiled, ½ cup	185
Kidney beans, boiled, 1 cup	713
Lentils, boiled, 1 cup	731
Mushrooms, boiled, ½ cup	277
Orange, 1 medium	250
Orange juice, 1 cup	496
Peaches, 1 medium	171
Potatoes, baked with skin, 1 medium	844
Prunes, dried, 10	626
Raisins, ¼ cup	280
Sunflower seeds, 1 ounce	196
Sweet potatoes, baked with skin, 1 medium	397
Tomatoes, 1 medium	273
Watermelon, 1 cup	186

All of these serving sizes are for raw foods, except for asparagus, black-eyed peas, broccoli, green beans, kidney beans, lentils, and mushrooms, all of which are boiled; dates and prunes, which are dried; and potatoes and sweet potatoes, which are baked and eaten with the skin. A bonus: All of these foods also are very low in sodium. That's not always the case, since foods that are high in potassium can also be high in sodium and in calories.

How much potassium is enough? Doctors recommend trying to get at least 3,500 milligrams a day. Unlike sodium, the more potassium you eat, the better. Getting your 3,500 milligrams is a cinch. A baked potato, a glass of orange juice, and a banana together provide more than half of the daily requirement.

In some cases, blood pressure medication can rob your body of potassium. This is true with a class of drugs called diuretics, commonly known as water pills. They're designed to make your kidneys flush extra water and salt from your body. Sometimes potassium goes out with the sodium. If this is a problem for you, your doctor may tell you to take potassium supplements. Or he may switch you to other types of diuretics called potassium-sparing. These help your body keep potassium while they flush the water and sodium. We'll talk about drugs in more detail in chapter 5.

THE DANGERS OF FAT

There's no denying it: Fat makes food taste good. It puts the mmm in muffins, the ahhh in avocados, and the sizzle in steak.

Unfortunately, a high-fat diet also clogs your arteries and puts you at risk for heart disease. People with hypertension already are more likely to have heart attacks, heart failure, and other problems. So eating too much fat can be a double-dip of danger.

In truth, fat isn't all bad. Your body needs it to function well. And it's a major source of energy. Every gram of fat that you burn provides nine calories of energy. That's more than twice as many calories per gram as carbohydrates.

The problem is that we don't always know when to say enough. Fat tastes good, so we like to eat it—often way too much of it. That's when the trouble starts. Weight gain. High cholesterol. Clogged arteries. So cut back on your fat intake now!

Most doctors recommend that you get no more than 30 percent of your daily calories in the form of fat. That means if you're on a 2,000-calorie diet, no more than 600 calories should come from fat. For a 2,500-calorie diet, the limit is about 750 calories.

Fat comes in two basic forms: saturated and unsaturated. Saturated fat comes from meat and other animal products such as cheese, whole milk, and lard. You'll also find it in tropical vegetable oils, such as palm and coconut. Saturated fat is generally considered bad because too much of it can lead directly to cardiovascular disease.

Unsaturated fats are often called good fats because, eaten in moderation, they can actually help reduce the cholesterol levels in your blood and fight heart disease. Unsaturated fats are divided into two categories: monounsaturated and polyunsaturated. Monounsaturated fat is the better of the two good fats because it reduces the level of LDL cholesterol (the bad kind) in your system and may increase the level of HDL cholesterol (the good cholesterol). It includes the oil found in avocados, as well as olive oil, canola oil, and almonds.

Polyunsaturated fat includes the fat found in corn oil, safflower oil, and walnuts. It helps reduce LDL cholesterol, too—but it can also lower HDL cholesterol (the good kind).

Remember: no more than 30 percent of your daily calories should come from fat. And no more than one-third of that should come from saturated fat. In fact, some doctors believe people with hypertension should limit themselves to 20 percent of calories from fat, with no more than one-third of that coming from saturated fat.

How do you get started on this low-fat lifestyle? Here are a few tips.

Check labels. The same food labels that tell how much sodium you're getting per serving also give the amounts of fat per serving. The fat is counted in grams.

If you're on a 2,000-calorie diet, you should aim for no more than 65 grams of fat a day. Of that total, no more than 20 grams should come from saturated fat. People on a 2,500-calorie diet should eat no more than 80 grams of fat a day, with no more than 25 grams coming from saturated fat.

Choose leaner meats. Fresh or smoked meats don't always come with labels, so it helps to know beforehand how much fat various cuts contain. This chart will help you make healthier choices.

Type	Serving Size	Total Fat	Saturated Fat
		(grams per serving)	
Beef *(trimmed of visible fat)*			
Ground, 10% fat	3 oz.	9.6	4.6
Ground, 21% fat	3 oz.	17.3	8.3
Rib roast, choice grade	3 oz.	11.4	5.5
Steak, flank	3 oz.	6.2	3.0
Steak, porterhouse	3 oz.	8.9	4.3
Steak, round	3 oz.	5.2	2.5
Steak, sirloin, choice grade	3 oz.	8.1	3.9
Steak, T-bone, meat only	3 oz.	8.8	4.2
Lamb *(trimmed of visible fat)*			
Leg	3 oz.	6.0	3.4
Loin chop	3 oz.	6.4	3.6

Type	Serving Size	Total Fat	Saturated Fat
		(grams per serving)	
Pork			
Pork loin	3 oz.	4.1	1.4
Bacon, thick	2 strips	12.5	4.0
Ham, fresh	3 oz.	8.5	3.1
Chicken *(roasted, skin removed)*			
Dark meat	3 oz.	5.4	1.7
Light meat	3 oz.	2.9	0.9
Turkey *(roasted, skin removed)*			
Dark meat	3 oz.	7.1	2.0
Light meat	3 oz.	3.3	1.0

(Source: United States Department of Agriculture)

When shopping for red meat, try to purchase lean or extra-lean cuts. Lean cuts have less than 10 grams of total fat per serving, including no more than 4 grams of saturated fat. Extra-lean cuts have 5 grams or less of total fat per serving, including no more than 2 grams of saturated fat.

Put fish on the menu. Fish is a great substitute for meat. It's low in saturated fat and cholesterol. It tastes great. It also has an important extra benefit: many types of fish contain omega-3 fatty acids, a form of polyunsaturated fat. While "fatty" and "acid" don't sound like a bonus, omega-3s may lower your risk of heart disease and reduce your blood pressure.

A study of African tribesmen found that people who eat a fish-heavy diet may actually be better off than those who eat nothing but vegetables. Researchers looked at more than 1,200 Bantu people, about half of whom ate mostly fish and half of whom ate mostly vegetables. The people who ate fish had an average systolic blood pressure reading of 122.6 mm Hg, while those who ate mostly rice and corn had an average reading of 132.6 mm Hg. The fish-eating people also had healthier cholesterol levels.

That's great news because fish is such an easy thing to add to your diet. Not all fish have the same levels of omega-3 fatty acids. The best sources include anchovies, mackerel, salmon, swordfish, and tuna. Be sure to rinse any canned fish in water to remove the salt that gets added during processing.

Don't believe the hype. Everybody is jumping on the low-fat bandwagon these days. Hundreds of products now claim to be nonfat or low-fat or reduced-fat. They all sound healthy, but be careful: The terms don't all mean the same thing.

Nonfat means what it says: There's little or no fat in the food. When you see this term on the label, you've got a winner. *Low-fat* is good, too: To claim this title, a food must have three grams or less of total fat and no more than one gram of saturated fat per serving.

Reduced-fat can be a little trickier to decipher, however. It means a food must have at least 25 percent less fat than a similar product. This certainly sounds good—but be careful. Say a salad dressing has 16 grams of fat per serving. If a manufacturer changes the ingredients so that the dressing has 12 grams of fat per serving, it can be labeled as a reduced-fat product. But at 12 grams of fat per serving, that salad dressing is still no bargain for your heart.

LOWERING CHOLESTEROL

It's impossible to talk about fat without mentioning cholesterol, too. After all, they go together like ham and cheese. Cholesterol is a waxy, fat-like substance that flows through your bloodstream. Like fat, it serves important functions in your body. But also like fat, too much cholesterol can cause serious damage. It can clog up your arteries, leading to blockages that cause heart disease and stroke.

We get cholesterol from two places: The liver produces small amounts, and foods supply a lot more. Like saturated fat, cholesterol is found in all types of animal products, from meat to milk. Fat and cholesterol are locked together in a dangerous little dance inside our bodies. If we eat too much saturated fat, our bodies produce more cholesterol than we really need. Then we make matters worse by getting too much cholesterol in our diets.

As we've seen, high cholesterol is a serious risk factor for cardiovascular disease. And since people with high blood pressure are already in danger of heart trouble, too much cholesterol can have a doubly dangerous effect on their health. Sadly, about 40 percent of people with hypertension also have high cholesterol levels.

How do you fight back? Well, the most powerful weapon is a low-fat diet. Eating less saturated fat causes your body to produce less cholesterol. But you can help matters even further by reducing the amount of cholesterol you eat every day. Be careful to decrease both saturated fat and cholesterol. While many foods are heavy in both, there are many foods rich in saturated fat but not cholesterol (and vice-versa).

WATCH OUT FOR THE McFAT

F-A-S-T food is F-A-T food. And the extra S stands for sodium. A typical meal at McDonald's—a Quarter Pounder with cheese, large fries, and a vanilla shake—will blow your whole fat and sodium budget for the day.

But let's be realistic here. Fast food has become a part of our lives. The grandkids are always begging for a trip to Burger King or Pizza Hut, and you can't always tell them no. So when you go, just be smart. Here's a quick list of main courses at some popular restaurant chains, along with the fat and sodium these foods contain:

FOOD	FAT (grams per serving)	SODIUM (milligrams per serving)
Arby's		
The Good		
Roast chicken salad	2	418
The Bad		
Regular roast beef	19	1,009
The Ugly		
Philly Beef N' Swiss	47	2,025
Roast beef sub	42	2,034
Burger King		
The Good		
Broiled chicken salad	10	110
The Bad		
Chicken tenders (8 pieces)	17	710
The Ugly		
Chicken sandwich	43	1,400
Whopper with cheese	46	1,350

FOOD	FAT (grams per serving)	SODIUM (milligrams per serving)
McDonald's		
The Good		
Grilled chicken salad	1.5	240
The Bad		
Grilled Chicken Deluxe	20	1,040
The Ugly		
Big Mac	31	1,070
Quarter Pounder with cheese	30	1,290
Pizza Hut		
The Not-Quite-Good		
Spaghetti with marinara sauce	6	730
The Bad		
Pan cheese pizza, 2 slices	18	940
The Ugly		
Personal Pan pepperoni pizza	30	1,363
Wendy's		
The Not-Quite-Good		
Grilled chicken sandwich	7	720
The Bad		
Single hamburger with the works	23	860
The Ugly		
Big Bacon Classic	36	1,500

(Source: Fast Food Facts, from the Minnesota Attorney General's Office)

Doctors say that you should get no more than 300 milligrams of cholesterol every day. Here's a list of common foods and the amounts of cholesterol they contain.

CHOLESTEROL COUNTS

Food	Cholesterol (milligrams per serving)
All fresh fruits and vegetables	0
Bagel, egg	8
Bagel, regular	0
Bran muffin	40
Butter, 2 tsp.	21
Cheese	
American, 1 oz.	26
Cheddar, 1 oz.	29
Cottage, low-fat, ½ cup	5
Cream, 1 oz.	31
Custard, ½ cup	139
Egg, large	211
Seafood	
Cod, 3 oz.	47
Flounder, 3 oz.	58
Squid, fried, 3 oz.	220
Shrimp, 3 oz.	166
Meat	
Chicken, breast, 3 oz.	73
Ham, 3 oz.	80
Lamb, leg, 3 oz.	76
Pâté, 1 oz.	43

Food	Cholesterol (milligrams per serving)
Steak, T-bone, 3 oz.	68
Turkey, dark meat, 3 oz.	72
Turkey, white meat, 3 oz.	39
Milk	
Skim, 8 oz.	4
Whole, 8 oz.	35

There's one more way to fight cholesterol: with fiber. Almost all high-fiber foods are low in fat (and, as a bonus, low in sodium). Less fat in your diet means less cholesterol in your blood. What's more, one type of fiber—soluble fiber—directly lowers your cholesterol count. You'll find high amounts of soluble fiber in beans, peas, berries, pears, oats, apples, carrots, and prunes.

Doctors recommend eating about 25 grams of fiber a day. Many breakfast cereals are high in fiber, as are these common foods.

FIBER COUNTS

Food	Fiber (grams per serving)
Apple, 1 medium	3.0
Chickpeas, ½ cup	7.0
Figs, 3 dried	5.2
Lima beans, ½ cup	6.8
Oatmeal, ¾ cup	3.9
Pear, 1 medium	4.3
Prunes, 5	3.0

Food	Fiber (grams per serving)
Raspberries, 1 cup	6.0
Spaghetti, 1 cup	2.2
Spaghetti, whole-wheat, 1 cup	5.4

THE BENEFITS OF CALCIUM

One of the hottest debates in blood pressure treatment right now is whether taking extra calcium can help. In many, but not all, studies, people who got low amounts of calcium had higher blood pressure levels than those who got normal amounts. Some researchers believe that getting too little calcium can make your body react badly to extra sodium.

There's little evidence that extra calcium will lower your blood pressure much, if at all. But you still need to meet your daily requirement. The recommended daily intake for men and women under age 50 is 1,000 milligrams. At age 50 and older, the daily requirement rises to 1,200 milligrams.

Almost all dairy products are high in calcium. An eight-ounce glass of skim milk, for example, has about 300 milligrams of calcium. But most dairy foods are also high in fat, so be sure to choose nonfat or low-fat varieties of cheese, yogurt, and other items. Here are a few other foods that are rich in calcium.

CALCIUM COUNTS

Food	Calcium (milligrams per serving)
Cheese, Swiss, 1 oz.	262
Collard greens, 1 cup cooked	220

Food	Calcium (milligrams per serving)
Kale, 1 cup cooked	206
Sardines, 2 ounces	248
Yogurt, low-fat plain, 1 cup	294

DASH YOUR WAY TO LOWER PRESSURE

For years, the story on food and high blood pressure was always the same: Eat fewer calories, drink less alcohol, and cut back on salt. Well, these factors are still important. But experts now know another secret about diet and hypertension: The types of food you eat can be as important as how much you eat. In fact, changing the types of food in your diet may help lower your blood pressure whether or not you lose weight.

This comes from an important piece of research called the DASH study. DASH stands for Dietary Approaches to Stop Hypertension. In this 11-week study, 459 adults were fed different diets.

For the first three weeks, everyone in the study ate a diet relatively low in fruits, vegetables, and dairy products. The amount of fat in the diet was typical for most Americans. After that three-week period, the group split up. Some people continued to eat the same diet. Others started on a high-fruit, high-vegetable diet. And a third group began eating the DASH diet: high in fruits, vegetables, and low-fat dairy products but low in fat. Doctors made sure that people in all three groups ate the same amount of salt. They also gave people enough food each day to keep them at the same weight throughout the study.

When 11 weeks had passed, it was time to check everyone's blood pressure. The high-fruit, high-vegetable diet did very well. Compared with the regular diet, it lowered systolic blood pressure by about 2.8 mm Hg and diastolic pressure by about 1.1 mm Hg.

But the clear winner in the study was the DASH diet. Compared with the regular diet, it lowered systolic pressure by about 5.5 mm Hg and diastolic pressure by about 3.0 mm Hg. Among those people who had hypertension at the start of the study, the effect was even more amazing: Systolic readings dropped by 11.4 mm Hg, and diastolic readings fell by 5.5 mm Hg.

These are powerful changes. For some people, switching to the DASH diet could be enough to completely eliminate the need for high blood pressure medicine.

Put the DASH Diet to Work

So how do you get started? First, understand the key point: The DASH diet doesn't make you stop eating anything. You can still have an occasional burger, brownie, or bowl of ice cream. But to make the diet work, you must eat more of certain types of foods—particularly vegetables, fruits, and low-fat dairy products.

Vegetables. You hated them as a child, but your heart will love them now. The DASH diet calls for four to five servings of vegetables per day. They're terrific sources of fiber and potassium, both of which may help lower your blood pressure. One serving equals 1 cup of a raw, leafy vegetable such as lettuce or kale, $1/2$ cup of a cooked vegetable, or six ounces of vegetable juice.

Everybody knows what a vegetable is, so there's no need to list them all. Just be sure to stop thinking of main and side dishes. Well-seasoned green beans can make a great main dish. Have an artichoke today and a sweet potato tomorrow. Supermarkets stock an enormous variety of fresh vegetables, so you can explore new tastes all the time. There's no reason to get bored when following the DASH diet.

Fruits. The DASH diet calls for four to five servings of fruits per day. You may be getting close to this amount already. Start your day with a six-ounce glass of orange or grapefruit juice and a banana, and you're halfway there. Add an apple or fruit juice at lunch and a nectarine or peach later on, and you've made it. One serving is a medium-size piece of fruit, $1/4$ cup of dried fruit, $1/2$ cup of frozen or canned fruit, or six ounces of juice. Again, don't hesitate to explore nature's bounty. Ever eat a mango?

Dairy. To get the benefits of dairy without the problems, always choose low-fat. Drink skim or 1 percent milk. Try nonfat or low-fat yogurt and low-fat cheeses such as part-skim mozzarella. Milk, cheese, and other dairy foods give you excellent amounts of calcium and protein. Shoot for two to three servings per day. A serving is eight ounces of milk, one cup of yogurt, or $11/2$ ounces of cheese.

Grains. Grains and grain products—whole wheat breads, pasta, cereals, oatmeal, and bagels—will be your main source of energy and fiber. In a 2,000-calorie diet, you need seven to eight servings of grains per day. A serving is one slice of bread or $1/2$ cup of cereal, or cooked rice or pasta.

Meats. Most of us were brought up to think of meat, poultry, and fish as main dishes. But in the DASH diet, meat is just another part of a meal—no more or less important or prominent than a side dish of string beans. This means you should be eating a lot less of it. In a typical 2,000-calorie diet, you should eat no more than two servings of meat per day. A serving is three ounces of meat, poultry, or fish. When picking a cut of meat, make sure it's lean. Before cooking, trim away any fat that you can see. And try to cook your meat in healthy ways, such as broiling, roasting, and boiling. Frying meat in oil adds fat and calories.

Nuts. Nuts and seeds (such as sunflower seeds) are great sources of potassium, protein, and energy. They're high in fiber, too. But because they're also high in fat, one serving every other day is plenty. A serving equals $1\frac{1}{2}$ ounces or $\frac{1}{3}$ cup of nuts or two tablespoons of seeds.

Ease into DASH

If you've ever been on a diet—and who hasn't?—you know it's not easy to make sudden changes in your diet. So don't even try. Instead, make gradual changes. Try a meatless dinner once in a while. Add an extra piece of fruit at lunchtime. And if you get a craving for sweets, try something low in fat and calories, such as sugar-free gelatin. After a few weeks, you should be ready to go all-out with your new DASH diet.

Here's a sample of a daily menu.

A DAY OF DASH

Food	Serving Size	Servings Equivalent
Breakfast		
Orange juice	6 oz.	1 fruit
Cornflakes with 1 tsp. sugar	1 cup	2 grains
1% milk	8 oz.	1 dairy
Whole-wheat toast with		
1 tbsp. jelly	1 slice	1 grain

Food	Serving Size	Servings Equivalent
Soft margarine	1 tsp.	1 fat
Lunch		
Chicken salad	¾ cup	1 meat
Pita bread	½ slice	1 grain
Raw vegetables		
carrots and celery	3-4 sticks each	1 vegetable
lettuce	2 leaves	1 vegetable
radishes	2	1 vegetable
Part-skim mozzarella cheese	1½ oz.	1 dairy
Fruit cocktail in light syrup	½ cup	1 fruit
1% milk	8 oz.	1 dairy
Dinner		
Herbed baked cod	3 oz.	1 meat
Scallion rice	1 cup	2 grains
Steamed broccoli	½ cup	1 vegetable
Stewed tomatoes	½ cup	1 vegetable
Spinach salad		
raw spinach	½ cup	1 vegetable
cherry tomatoes	2	1 vegetable
cucumbers	2 slices	1 vegetable
Light Italian dressing	1 tbsp.	½ fat
Whole-wheat roll	1 small	1 grain
Soft margarine	1 tsp.	1 fat
Melon balls	½ cup	1 fruit

Food	Serving Size	Servings Equivalent
Snacks		
Diet ginger ale	12 oz.	NA
Dried apricots	1 oz.	1 fruit
Mini-pretzels	1 oz.	1 grain
Mixed nuts	1½ oz.	1 nuts

Looks pretty tasty, doesn't it? It's certainly better than an all-mushroom diet or some other crazy plan. The DASH diet can be your first step toward lower blood pressure. You may not get the exact same results as the people in the study, but that's not really the point. You're starting to take charge of your health.

One last thing about the DASH diet: Although the people in the study remained at the same weight, that doesn't mean you should, too. The doctors wanted to make sure that the blood pressure changes were due to the types of foods the people ate, not the amount of weight they lost. In reality, you may double the diet's benefit by eating the right foods and losing weight at the same time.

PUTTING IT ALL TOGETHER

Changing the way you eat isn't always easy. After all, you've been eating this way for years and years.

But if you really want to lower your blood pressure—or keep it from getting high in the first place—you're going to have to face the food issue. You're going to have to look your refrigerator in the eye and say, "Enough is enough! I'm taking charge here!"

The key to changing your diet is to do it slowly. You have lots of old habits to break and lots of new ones to make. It's not realistic to try to cut out fat, cholesterol, and sodium all in one day. And it's just as unwise to try to add fiber, potassium, and all of those other goodies at the same time. (Be especially careful about adding too much fiber too soon. If your digestive system isn't used to it, fiber can flow through you like a flood.)

Take your time. Learn to enjoy new foods. Don't feel like you're giving up rocky road ice cream forever; you can still have some once in a while. As time passes, you'll find your cravings for fat slowly disappearing. You'll forget about that saltshaker you gave to the Salvation Army. And— believe it or not—you may find yourself looking forward to that morning bowl of oatmeal. Eventually, the DASH diet we've been talking about will feel as natural as taking an afternoon nap in a hammock.

Here are some additional tips to help you gently slide into your healthier lifestyle.

Love your legumes. Beans are good for your heart. So try to include beans or peas in your meals at least a few times each week. Beans come in all sizes, colors, and tastes. They're easy to add to salads. And they're a great substitute for meat in chilies, soups, and stews. Just beware of canned beans: They're usually packed in salty water. Rinsing them well will help reduce the sodium.

Pass on the packages. Big problems can come in small containers. A bag of potato chips can have a day's worth of sodium and fat. So can tortilla chips or flavored pop-corn. Even the low-fat varieties can be swimming in salt. Instead, try out some unsalted hard pretzels. Or air-pop some popcorn and flavor it with something like a dash of Parmesan cheese.

Go easy on the oil. Why fry? Any time you cook something in butter or oil, you're adding tons of fat and needless calories. Instead of frying your meat or fish, try to bake, broil, or grill it. The same goes for vegetables. Try steaming them, roasting them, or stir-frying them in chicken broth. If you just can't put down the frying pan, try using a nonfat cooking spray instead of oil. And if you can't avoid oil, pick olive or canola oil, which contains healthier fats than butter. Use as little oil as possible.

Spread lightly. Top your toast with something other than butter. Maybe a little jam or honey will satisfy you. If you're a real maniac for margarine, check your supermarket for reduced-fat varieties. None of the stuff is really good for you—but some brands may have only 2 to 6 grams of fat per tablespoon, which is much better than the 10-plus grams per tablespoon of butter.

Can't say no to mayo or sour cream? Try out the nonfat varieties. Just be sure to check the label for sodium. And remember: Nonfat doesn't mean no calories. Many nonfat and low-fat foods are still high in calories, which isn't good for your blood pressure or your waistline.

Go ahead, eat meat. We're not taking away all of your fun. Just cut back to two servings per day. A typical serving is $3\frac{1}{2}$ to 4 ounces, a piece that looks about as big as a deck of playing cards.

Choose skinless chicken over red meat or pork when you get the chance. It's lower in fat. When you do indulge in beef, know your cuts. Cuts such as round, tenderloin, top loin, and sirloin are less fatty when they're graded as select rather than as prime or choice.

When you're talking turkey, remember that white meat is less fatty than dark meat. And cold cuts such as turkey breast, lean ham, and lean roast beef are your best choices—but they're almost always high in sodium, so take it easy.

Take advantage of dairy. Dairy foods are important sources of calcium, protein, and other nutrients, so don't ignore them. Just switch from high-fat items such as cream and whole milk to less-fatty choices such as skim or 1 percent milk. Pick part-skim mozzarella cheese. And always choose nonfat or low-fat options when it comes to yogurt, cream cheese, and cottage cheese.

If you're craving a high-fat cheese such as Brie, do it on a day when you're not eating meat. That way, you won't overload your system with saturated fat.

Then there are eggs. Medical scientists and egg lobbyists have gone round and round over whether eggs cause harm. There's no question that they have cholesterol in them—more than 200 milligrams each. You don't have to completely eliminate them from your diet, however. Most people can eat two or three a week without exceeding the recommended limit of 300 milligrams of cholesterol per day.

EXTRA PROTECTION

Good nutrition doesn't come in a bottle. It comes from eating the right foods. But many people believe that they can improve their diets—and help fight diseases such as hypertension and heart disease at the same time—with the help of nutritional supplements. While the evidence is still hazy, some of the early research seems promising.

Two of the most popular compounds are vitamin C and vitamin E. They're also called antioxidants because they help your body get rid of free radicals—oxygen molecules that cause LDL cholesterol to stick to the walls of your arteries. This can cause blockages that can lead directly to heart attack, blood clots, and other deadly problems. Whether antioxidants help prevent such blockages from occurring is a topic of great interest to scientists and the general public.

Since people with high blood pressure already are more likely to develop atherosclerosis, or hardening of the arteries, it makes sense to pay close attention to antioxidants. Fortunately, eating a good, balanced diet is the best way to load up on antioxidants. Fruits and vegetables are great sources of vitamin C and beta-carotene.

Some people are convinced that taking high-dose supplements will help even more. But the jury is still out on this one. In fact, recent research has suggested that taking supplements of beta-carotene actually increases the risk of lung cancer among people who smoke. This may not pertain to you, but the point is that we just don't have enough data yet to say what is good and what isn't. In general, it's best to get vitamin C and beta-carotene from your diet, especially from fruits and vegetables.

The story about vitamin E is a bit different. The evidence in favor of taking vitamin E supplements is stronger. Some doctors believe that high doses of vitamin E can lower your risk of heart disease. But the amount needed is far more than you can get in your everyday diet. Most people get about 10 international units of vitamin E in their diets each day. The amount needed for heart protection may be 400 international units per day. If you want to try vitamin E supplements for heart protection, please speak to your doctor first. Large doses of vitamin E aren't for everybody—especially people who are taking blood-thinning medications.

Research will continue on supplements, of course. And new claims about miracle foods will come and go with each week's supermarket tabloid. But sometimes a real find will surface, and it could make your life a whole lot better.

Here's an example: A doctor wrote in a popular medical journal that he had a patient whose blood pressure dropped by a huge amount—46 mm Hg systolic and 13 mm Hg diastolic—after the man drank a six-ounce glass of grapefruit juice every day for a year. It turns out that grapefruit juice has flavonoids, compounds that may have boosted the effects of the man's blood pressure medication. Of course, your case may be entirely different from his. But don't be afraid to ask your doctor about new diet findings that may help you, too.

THINK BEFORE YOU DRINK

Let's end our diet discussion the way you might finish a meal at a fancy French restaurant—with an after-dinner drink and a cup of coffee. Talk about your highs and lows. The alcohol in your amaretto is a depressant. It can dull your senses and your reactions, making you groggy and lethargic. The caffeine in your coffee, on the other hand, is liquid lightning. It shoots through your system like an electric pulse, making you more energetic.

While alcohol and coffee couldn't be more different in the ways they act on your body, they do have one side effect in common: Both can raise your blood pressure. So if you use one or both, it may be time to cut back a little.

Doctors aren't completely sure how caffeine raises blood pressure. Their best guess right now is that it constricts your blood vessels. This means your blood must flow through smaller openings, which makes your heart pump harder. A single cup of coffee can boost your systolic and diastolic blood pressure readings by five mm Hg each. This is true whether or not you have hypertension.

Fortunately, it's a temporary effect. Caffeine's effects peak about one hour after you ingest it and usually are pretty much gone about two hours after that. So if you drink only one cup of coffee a day, you don't have anything to worry about, right?

Well, maybe. But most of us don't stop after that early-morning jolt of java. We guzzle cup after cup throughout the day. And what we call a cup is more like a bathtub with a handle—12, 24, even 36 ounces. As a result, our blood pressure readings can stay higher hour after hour.

Your body does build a little short-term tolerance for caffeine. Drinking three cups in a row won't raise your blood pressure three times as much as one cup. But this tolerance doesn't carry on for very long. When you wake up in the morning, most of the caffeine in your system is gone—and your blood pressure is in for another hit.

One recent study showed that giving up caffeine for good can help reduce high blood pressure. Researchers looked at a group of healthy, nonsmoking men who drank about four cups of coffee a day. The men were asked to drink the same brand of coffee for two months. Then their blood pressure was measured. Two types of readings were taken: resting pressure and ambulatory pressure (blood pressure that is taken at different points throughout the day and night).

The men split up into three groups. One group kept drinking the same type and amount of coffee. Another switched to decaffeinated coffee. The third went cold turkey and gave up coffee. After two months, doctors took resting and ambulatory blood pressure readings again.

The resting blood pressure readings didn't differ much among the three groups. But the men who cut out caffeine—either by drinking decaf or by not drinking any coffee—had significantly lower ambulatory blood pressure readings. On average, their systolic readings were three to five mm Hg lower, while their diastolic readings were two to three mm Hg lower.

That may not seem like a huge difference, maybe not even enough to make you give up coffee. But you have to keep in mind that even small reductions in blood pressure can make a big difference. It could mean reducing the amount of medicine you have to take. Or—if you combine it with weight loss, a better diet, and other factors—it could mean controlling your blood pressure without medication.

Besides, there are other reasons to cut back on coffee. For one thing, it has no nutritional value at all. Despite its reputation as a pick-me-up, it doesn't really make you sharper or more productive at the office. And there's even evidence that drinking boiled coffee can raise the cholesterol levels in the blood. Drinking typical American coffee, which is filtered, not boiled, probably has no effect on cholesterol.

Just cutting back on coffee may not solve your caffeine problem, however. Lots of other things we eat and drink contain caffeine. Here's a short list.

CAFFEINE COUNTS

Foods and Beverages	Caffeine (milligrams per serving)
Chocolate, baking, 1 oz.	25
Chocolate, bittersweet, 1 oz.	20
Cocoa, 6 oz.	5
Coffee, brewed, 6 oz.	100

Foods and Beverages	Caffeine (milligrams per serving)
Coffee, decaffeinated, 6 oz.	2
Coffee, instant, 6 oz.	55-60
Cola, 12 oz.	40-50
Tea, 6 oz.	35-40

There's no standard for how much caffeine is too much. It's just a good idea to cut back where you can, because every little bit helps.

The same advice holds true if you're an alcohol drinker. For many people with hypertension, alcohol may play a key role. Experts believe that about 7 percent of cases of hypertension are related to heavy alcohol consumption.

What's considered heavy? Three or more drinks a day. A drink is defined as one bottle of beer with a 4.5 percent alcohol content, a 4-ounce glass of wine with a 12 percent alcohol content, or a 1-ounce shot of 80-proof liquor.

If you're drinking this much alcohol, cutting back a little can make a significant difference in your blood pressure. In one study, researchers looked at men ages 30 to 59, all of whom had blood pressure between 140 and 179 mm Hg systolic and 90 and 109 mm Hg diastolic. After cutting back from four drinks to two, the average man in the study had a 3.6 mm Hg drop in systolic pressure.

Alcohol isn't all bad. Doctors have found that drinking in moderation can actually help your cholesterol. It can lower the level of LDL, the "bad" cholesterol, and increase the level of HDL, the "good" cholesterol, in your bloodstream. Studies also show that moderate drinkers have a slightly lower risk of heart attack.

But we can't toast these findings without a couple of words of warning. First, you have to drink in moderation. No more than two drinks a day. Anything more than that will do just the opposite of what you want: It will increase your blood pressure and your risk of heart disease. Second, these findings really aren't a strong enough reason to start drinking if you don't already. On average, people who don't drink are pretty healthy—so why mess around with a good thing?

As you can see, you don't always need a high-tech approach to beat hypertension. We hope this chapter has given you lots of food for thought about natural ways to help lower your blood pressure.

CHAPTER 4

Handling Hypertension by Helping Your Heart

In the previous chapter, you learned how making a few changes in your diet can really rein in your blood pressure. You may even have discovered a few simple pleasures, like how good a chilled grapefruit tastes first thing in the morning. Or how less salt and more spices really perk up a piece of pork. Or how good it feels to slip into slacks that have been hanging in the basement closet since Jimmy Carter was president.

You've earned a pat on the back. So congratulate yourself. And get ready to make things even better.

The main topics we're going to talk about in this chapter—exercising and quitting smoking—are extremely important for your heart. Remember, people with high blood pressure have a much higher risk of heart attack, heart failure, stroke, and other serious conditions. If you add extra risk factors such as lack of exercise or smoking, the problems with your heart can get much, much worse.

We'll begin by talking about easy ways to get light exercise. Then we'll move on to moderate workouts that can really make a difference. Along the way, we'll throw in

BIGGER ISN'T BETTER

Lifestyle changes like a better diet and more exercise can help improve a serious heart condition called left ventricular hypertrophy. The left ventricle is the largest chamber in your heart. Its job is to pump blood out of the heart and into the arteries. When your blood pressure is too high, this puts extra strain on the left ventricle. Like any muscle, it compensates by growing larger. While this might sound like a good thing, it isn't. The heart muscle can't get enough blood to feed itself—and this can lead to chest pain (angina), heart attacks, irregular heartbeats, and congestive heart failure.

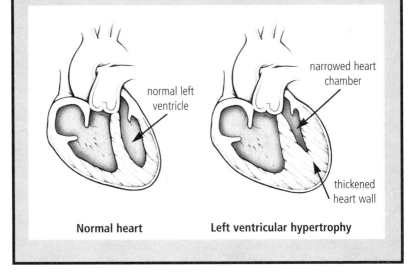

Normal heart **Left ventricular hypertrophy**

information about stretching, warming up, cooling down, and a few other important workout tips. And we'll tell you about sneaky ways to grab a little exercise starting right now.

If you smoke, you have probably promised yourself a hundred times that you're going to quit. Right after the holidays. Or when you retire. Or when the Cubs or Red

Sox win the World Series. Maybe you even have stopped, only to slip back into the habit after a few weeks or months. Well, you'll never have a better reason to quit than high blood pressure. And there will never be a better time to quit than now.

It's easier to quit today than it has ever been. With all of the special gums, patches, and medications that are now available, you can get the boost you need to succeed. You can survive the cravings. You can learn to break that cigarette-and-cup-of-coffee habit. With the right tools, you can become a nonsmoker and save yourself thousands of dollars every year. And you can save yourself from some horrible health problems later.

Stress, of course, is nearly impossible to avoid. What you can do is learn to deal with it better. But let's not kid ourselves. Dealing with stress, quitting smoking, and getting exercise take effort. Nothing in life is free. Still, you have a perfect chance to make a difference in your life. You can take control of your health. You can feel better than you've ever felt—and maybe add years to your life right now.

But it all comes back to you. You have to want to do it. You have to want to change. Without that inner commitment, it's simply not going to happen. No amount of support from your doctor, spouse, siblings, or friends is going to make the difference.

So before you read any further, take a few minutes to reflect. Think about your goals. Think about your dreams. Think about the people near and dear to you. Think about what a great opportunity you have right here, right now, to make yourself healthier.

Then get started on your new lifestyle.

PUMP IT UP, PUMP IT DOWN

About half of all people with hypertension are sedentary. In everyday language, this means they don't move a whole lot. If your idea of exercise is a 10-yard dash to the refrigerator during television commercials, it's probably time to look a little more closely at how healthy regular exercise can be.

There's little question that exercise can help lower blood pressure whether or not you lose weight. Combined with a diet that's suited to your weight goals, moderate workouts can give body fat the heave-ho in a hurry. Both diet and exercise are important. It's hard to lose weight unless you cut back on calories and increase your physical activity.

Exercise does more than just help you lose weight. Doctors aren't quite sure why, but getting moderate—and perhaps even low—amounts of exercise seems to lower blood pressure in many people whether or not they lose a single pound. It also doesn't matter how heavy you are when you begin exercising; overweight or skinny, you're likely to see your blood pressure drop.

However exercise works, it clearly works very well. In a recent six-month study, men and women ages 60 to 85 who combined weight loss with reduced sodium intakes and more exercise experienced significant drops in blood pressure. Their systolic readings fell an average of 8.7 mm Hg, and their diastolic readings fell an average of 6.8 mm Hg.

There are two main types of exercise: isometric and isotonic. Isometric exercise is basically weight lifting; you work your muscles against some kind of resistance, such as a barbell or a Nautilus machine. Isometric exercises strengthen muscles. But they can sharply raise your blood pressure during a workout, even if they make you more fit in the long run. For this reason, many doctors recommend that you stay away from weight lifting if you have hypertension. It's not clear whether these spikes in blood pressure do more harm than good. Note: If you're already doing isometric exercises, talk to your doctor about whether it's wise to continue. She may think it's okay, since you've already developed a foundation of fitness. Using less weight and doing more repetitions may be a good compromise.

Isotonic exercises, also called dynamic exercises, are the ones that do the most good for people who are trying to lower their blood pressure. Isotonic exercises involve using your large muscles—especially those in your legs—to move your body. This can take many forms, from running and walking to swimming, bicycling, gardening, or even ballroom dancing. Isotonic exercises make your heart pump faster and your lungs work harder to deliver oxygen to your muscles. This makes them both stronger and more efficient. When they're in good shape, less effort is required to do everyday tasks, which reduces strain on your circulatory system.

As we've seen, weight loss is one of the biggest benefits of exercise. But why does exercise help? Well, mainly because exercise requires energy. It takes more energy to walk around the block than it does to watch a rerun of *The Beverly Hillbillies*. To get this extra energy, your body burns more calories. It gets these calories from one of two places: the foods you eat or the fat your body stores. If you burn more calories than you eat, your body uses its fat to make up the difference. And you'll become lighter!

Exercise can also change how your body handles calories even when you're not exercising. After a workout, your body will burn more calories throughout the day. So when you've finished your walk, you can watch Granny and Uncle Jed and still use extra calories while you flop on the sofa.

In the previous chapter, we talked about how cutting calories can help you lose weight. If you reduce your calorie intake by 500 a day, you're probably going to lose about one pound a week. Well, that's looking at the issue from only one side. Turn it around for a minute. If you burn more calories every day and combine that with eating less, you'll find it even easier to lose weight. Here's a chart that shows just how many calories some activities burn.

Activity	Calories Burned per 30 Minutes	
	123-lb Woman	*170-lb Man*
Aerobics (low-impact)	240	315
Basketball	231	318
Bicycling (5.5 mph)	108	147
Jogging (5.2 mph)	228	300
Racquetball	228	321
Running (8 min/mile)	339	450
Sitting	30	42
Stair-climbing (on a machine)	264	366
Swimming (slow crawl)	285	390
Tennis (singles)	183	243
Walking (4 mph)	132	183

Of course, these numbers vary from person to person. One person's idea of tennis may be leisurely lobbing the ball back and forth, while another person's may be playing a five-set match against Jimmy Connors. Still, the chart clearly shows one thing: Exercise really burns calories.

But we're getting a little ahead of ourselves. If you haven't exercised for a while, you're not going to start off running marathons or playing tennis at Wimbledon. More likely (and more sensibly), you're going to begin with a gentle stroll around the block. And that's terrific. Because people who move from doing no exercise to doing just a little may get the most benefit. The first step is the most important one of all.

One more thing: Before you begin any new exercise, schedule an appointment with your doctor. It's extremely important that he approves your program. After all, if you have hypertension, your blood pressure is already too high. It is likely to rise a little more while you're exercising (even though it will be lower the rest of the time). You need to make sure that your system can handle the extra load. It's not likely to be a problem, but you're always better off making sure ahead of time.

CHOOSING YOUR ACTIVITY

To make an exercise plan work, you have to like what you're doing. So take a minute to think. Do you enjoy quiet, solitary strolls through the woods? Would you rather join a class, where you can meet other people interested in fitness? How about a little bit of both? What about ballroom dancing? Or swimming? Or machines such as stair-climbers and treadmills?

There's a whole world of options to choose from. Pick one or two or three that you like. Just make sure that your activity matches your physical needs. If you have arthritic knees, for example, jogging and high-impact aerobic dancing probably aren't for you. One of the best workouts for people who have joint pain or who are overweight is swimming. It puts very little strain on the knees, hips, and shoulders, and it gives a first-class workout. Researchers at the University of Tennessee found that people who had high blood pressure were able to reduce their readings by 7 mm Hg systolic and 3 mm Hg diastolic just by taking a leisurely 45-minute swim three times a week for 10 weeks.

Walking is a great choice, too. Even people with bad ankles, knees, or hips can often walk without much trouble. And talk about a super way to meet people: Have you noticed how many men and women walk for fitness in parks and malls these days? You might even be able to join a walking club in your area. The more support you get from other people, the more likely you are to stick with your exercise program.

Whichever activity you choose, the next step is to figure out how hard to go at it. As we've seen, the objective of isotonic exercise is to get your heart and lungs working. This gives you an aerobic workout (aerobic means "with oxygen"). The point of aerobic exercise is to train your body to deliver oxygen and other nutrients to your cells more efficiently, so your heart won't have to work as hard to do its job.

You have three things to consider when deciding how to exercise: intensity, duration, and frequency. Intensity refers to how fast you make your heart beat. Basically, the faster the beat, the more benefit you get. But this doesn't mean you should start off trying to make your pulse race like a Corvette. If you're just beginning a workout routine, a moderate pace is the way to go.

Before you can determine the appropriate intensity, you have to figure out what your maximum heart rate is. To do this, just subtract your age from 220. If you're 50, 220 minus 50 equals 170. So your maximum heart rate is about 170 beats per minute.

Once you arrive at this number, you have to decide how intense your workout should be. Most people who are just starting out should aim for 50 to 70 percent of their maximum heart rate (this is considered moderate intensity). If your maximum heart rate is 170, multiply 170 by 0.5 to get 50 percent of maximum or by 0.7 to get 70 percent of maximum. In this case, 50 percent is 85 beats per minute, and 70 percent is about 120 beats per minute.

Here's a chart to make things easier.

Age	Maximum Heart Rate	50% of Maximum	70% of Maximum
30	190	95	135
35	185	95	130
40	180	90	125
45	175	90	125
50	170	85	120
55	165	85	115
60	160	80	110
65	155	80	110
70	150	75	105

Now you have to figure out how to measure your heart rate. There are two basic ways. One is to check your pulse at your wrist. Place the tips of the index and middle fingers of your right hand gently across the underside of your left wrist, just below the thumb. Move your fingers around a little until you can feel your pulse. Don't squeeze too hard, or you won't get a good reading. Using the second hand on your watch, count the number of beats for 15 seconds.

STICKING WITH IT

Starting an exercise program may be the hardest thing of all. But for most people, continuing an exercise program is the second hardest. There's that old rule of physics: A body at rest tends to stay at rest. Unless you're careful, it's very easy to slip back into the same sedentary routine. That's why you need a few tricks to help keep you going.

Remember why you're doing this. Exercise makes you healthier. It helps you fight high blood pressure. It can protect you against heart disease, stroke, and other problems. This is not some here-today, gone-tomorrow thing we're talking about. This is your life.

So when it's drizzling outside, or you're a little tired, or there's a new TV show you want to catch, don't give in to the temptation to blow off your workout. Wear a rain jacket. Tape the show. And get out there and make yourself healthy.

Set your schedule. Something will always get in the way of exercise if you let it. That's why you need to make your workout time a routine part of your day. Don't find time for exercise—make time for it. Write it in your daily planner: "12 p.m.-1 p.m.: Walking." Put a note on the refrigerator: "Dear husband/wife/kids/grandkids: I will be taking my daily walk from 3 p.m. to 4 p.m." Or tell your friends: "I'd love to go shopping with you Saturday. Let's do it after I'm done with my walk. How's one o'clock?"

Exercise is important. Treat it that way. And make sure the people in your life give it the same respect you do.

Exercise with a buddy. There always seems to be a reason to cancel a workout—bad weather, a headache, important errands. But when your exercise partner shows up at your door, it's harder to say no.

Don't expect perfection. Exercise will certainly make you healthier. But it won't necessarily turn you into a bronzed god or goddess. Losing weight and improving your fitness level will make you feel better and will probably give you more energy. Be happy with that. Don't be heartbroken if you don't end up as a size six. Who cares? You are who you are. And that's plenty good enough.

Mix it up. Nothing can wreck an exercise routine faster than boredom. So keep things fresh. If you're walking in your neighborhood, make a left turn at the corner instead of a right. Or hop in the car and drive to a park for a change of scenery. If you're getting a little tired of walking, try swimming. Or bicycling. You can choose from dozens of safe, enjoyable activities. There's no reason to get in a rut.

Take it easy. As you improve your fitness, you'll be tempted to increase your workout load. Not so fast! If you go too hard too soon, you're going to get hurt. And that can bring your exercise routine to a screeching halt. Don't ever push yourself past what is comfortable. There's plenty of time to improve. The most important thing is to stay in the game.

Multiply that number by 4 and you have the number of beats per minute. Twenty beats in 15 seconds? Multiply 20 by 4, and you have 80 beats per minute.

It's smart to practice this a little before you try it during a workout. A typical resting pulse is in the 70 to 85 range. So if that's what you get when you practice, you're probably doing it right.

The other way to measure your pulse is with a meter that straps around your chest. This will do the math for you. All you have to do is check the meter once in a while to make sure that you're staying within your limit. Some of these meters even come with a little bell that rings when your heartbeat goes too fast or too slow. You can purchase these meters in most sporting goods stores and drugstores.

That's all there is to know about intensity. Pick the level at which you want to keep your heart beating. If you find that your pulse is going too fast, slow down a little. On the other hand, if you find that your pulse has dropped below your zone, you need to speed up a bit.

There's one other way to measure intensity that's a little less scientific but a whole lot easier. It's called the talk test. If you find that you can hold a normal conversation while you're exercising, you know that you're not going too fast. If you are gasping for breath or breathing out of your mouth too much to talk properly, slow down a little.   .

One more word of caution is in order. It's vital that you talk to your doctor about choosing the right intensity. Your doctor will be able to tell you what pace is best for you, given your special needs and condition. The 50 to 70 percent guideline is just a general suggestion.

Now let's move on to duration. If intensity means "How hard?" then duration means "How long?" Once you reach your target pulse, you need to stay there for a little while to help your heart and lungs get stronger. To get the most from your workout, try to stay in your target zone for at least 30 minutes. This doesn't count the time you take to warm up or cool down. Start counting when your pulse reaches your target.

Thirty minutes per workout is plenty. As time goes by, you may feel like increasing to 45 minutes or even longer. It's not necessary. Your heart will be more than happy with the 30 minutes you give it.

Finally, we come to frequency. This is the "How often?" part. The quick answer: at least four times a week. And try to space out the days at first so that you take it easy on your body. If you are overweight or haven't exercised for a while, your body may not take well to the extra pounding. Going every other day gives you a little time to recover between workouts.

Having said that, please understand that you don't need to completely sit on your duff on the off-days. You can find plenty of ways to sneak in a little extra exercise. Walk up a flight or two of stairs instead of taking the elevator. Park farther from the entrance to the grocery store so that you get a little longer stroll. Or take the dogs for a bonus walk of 10 to 15 minutes. They'll love you for it.

Here are a few no-sweat exercises you can do every day and the amount of calories they burn.

GET IT WHERE YOU CAN: CALORIES BURNED PER 20 MINUTES

Activity	Your Weight		
	125 lb	*150 lb*	*175 lb*
Gardening	82	98	114
Shopping	70	84	98
Taking the stairs	300	350	404
Walking the dog (4 mph)	88	104	122

GETTING STARTED

Hold it! It's not healthy to just lace up your sneakers and burst out the door. Before you begin any activity, it's a good idea to warm up for 5 to 10 minutes. This gets your blood flowing a little bit and gives your heart a gentle jump-start. Take a few deep breaths. Get on your feet and pace back and forth. Try a couple of light stretches to get your joints limber and ready.

If you're a walker, stretch out those calf muscles. Stand facing a wall, about 12 inches away. Put your left foot about 12 to 20 inches behind you, flat on the floor. Slowly lean toward the wall, bending your right knee but keeping your left leg straight and your left foot flat. Brace yourself against the wall by putting your hands in front of your chest. You should feel a little stretch in your left calf. That's good. Hold it for about 30 seconds. Then do the same thing with your right leg.

You can also do a hamstring stretch to loosen up the backs of your upper legs. The easiest way to do this is the old touch-your-toes routine. Bend at the waist and slowly reach down toward your feet. Go only as far as is comfortable. Hold the stretch for maybe 20 seconds, then straighten up. Never bounce up and down when you're stretching.

When you're done with your workout, take another 5 to 10 minutes to cool down. Do the same stretches. Pace a little more until you feel that your heart rate and breathing have returned to normal. This will keep your muscles loose and limber, so you won't have pain later.

That's all there is to it. You've become an exerciser. You have picked the right exercises for you, and you're doing them at the right pace and with the right frequency. Within a couple of weeks, you'll probably notice the difference. You'll feel more energized. You might find yourself in a better mood. Most importantly, your blood pressure could be on its way down for good.

It really doesn't matter when you get your exercise. If your schedule allows it only after work, that's fine. But if you can find a way to sneak it in before you head to the office, you might benefit even more. That's because exercise tends to lower your blood pressure the most during the first five hours after your workout. Since your blood pressure usually rises to its peak during working hours, some doctors feel you're better off getting that five hours of help when you need it most—when you're on the job.

LIGHTS OUT: STOP SMOKING FOR GOOD

Every time you puff on a cigarette, your blood pressure shoots up like smoke through a chimney. Two cigarettes can raise your readings by about 10 mm Hg systolic and 8 mm Hg diastolic.

It's true that the effect doesn't last for long. After about 15 minutes, your pressure returns to normal. But think about it: If you smoke two packs a day, that's a total of 40 cigarettes. That's 40 blood pressure "ups" every 24 hours. If you smoke throughout the day, your blood pressure readings can spike higher than normal hour after hour after hour.

Besides, that's only part of the story. The real problem is that smoking is a major risk factor for heart disease. If you already have hypertension, adding smoking to your list of risks makes you a serious candidate for a heart attack.

If you're a smoker, you've probably been bombarded with statistics before. Let's look at some of the most important, courtesy of the American Lung Association:

- More than 430,000 Americans die every year from smoking-related diseases, including those who have heart attacks.
- Cigarettes contain at least 43 cancer-causing chemicals.
- Smoking during pregnancy is responsible for 20 to 30 percent of all low-birth-weight babies.
- Secondhand smoke is very dangerous for children. It causes between 150,000 and 300,000 cases of lower respiratory infections in children every year.

- More American women die annually from lung cancer than from breast cancer.
- In addition to cancer and heart disease, smoking can also cause infertility, slow wound healing, and stomach ulcers.

When it comes to heart disease and hypertension, you can control some risks but not others (such as heredity). Smoking is definitely one you can take care of. If you've just been diagnosed with hypertension, this is the excuse you need to quit smoking for good. You can do it. There are nearly 50 million former smokers out there. And there are another 33 million people who want to become former smokers. Maybe it's time to join the crowd.

Luckily for you, there's a lot more help available than there used to be. You don't have to go cold turkey anymore. You have your choice of prescription and nonprescription products that can help ease your transition.

Nicotine gums. Nicotine is the chemical that smokers crave. It's a stimulant, making you more alert. So if you trade in the nicotine in cigarettes for the nicotine in special gums, you can ease your craving for cigarettes. And you'll avoid all of the smoke and tar from cigarettes in the process.

Gums come in different strengths. The two-milligram version is for people who smoke fewer than 25 cigarettes a day. The four-milligram version is for those who smoke that many or more. Both types are now available without a prescription.

Nicotine gum is not a permanent solution. You'll need to taper off the gum as your cigarette cravings disappear. Here are some basic rules from the American Lung Association.

- Don't smoke once you start using the gum.

- Chew each piece slowly, making it last for about 30 minutes. If you slip the piece between your cheek and gum, the nicotine will be absorbed easier.
- Chew enough gum to handle the cravings, but don't go nuts. Ten to 15 pieces a day should be enough. Never use more than 30 pieces in a day.
- Use the gum each day for about a month. Then start tapering off slowly. Chew it only when you feel a craving.
- Quit chewing the gum altogether after about three months.

Nicotine patches. These are adhesive patches that deliver nicotine through your skin. They usually stick to your upper arm, under your shirtsleeve. Bigger patches deliver more nicotine than smaller ones.

Unlike gum, the patch delivers a constant flow of nicotine. This can make it easier to give up the patch when you're done. And it lessens some of the side effects that people often feel when they quit smoking, such as drowsiness and irritability. *Don't* smoke while you're wearing a patch, or you may experience nicotine overload that could even cause a heart attack.

Some people have side effects when they start using the patch. These can include headache, dizziness, upset stomach, weakness, blurred vision, vivid dreams, diarrhea, and some mild itching or burning at the site where you stick the patch.

No-nicotine drugs. The federal government recently approved the use of an antidepressant to help stop nicotine withdrawal symptoms. The drug is called bupropion hydrochloride; one brand name is Zyban. This prescription medication comes in pill form. It releases its active ingredient slowly to work against your cravings over the course of

STRESS: NOT WHAT IT'S CRACKED UP TO BE

It sure seems to make sense. Shouldn't stress cause high blood pressure? We've heard it repeated so many times that most of us just assume it's true. But the fact is that scientific studies have never shown any consistent link between stress and sustained high blood pressure.

There's no doubt that stress, like smoking, can raise blood pressure in the short run. Your body is designed to respond to stress by elevating your heart rate and pumping extra hormones, adrenaline and noradrenaline, into your bloodstream. These "stress hormones" make you alert and ready for action. Now this was great for cavemen, who sometimes had to sprint away from angry, charging beasts. But it's not so great for people today. Jumping up from our office chairs and leaping into the nearest tree just isn't a socially accepted way to deal with stress.

Research shows that it's not a stressful environment but how we respond to stress that's important to our blood pressure. Doctors looking at 654 men and women who worked in an Australian government tax office (how's that for stress?) found that those who used positive methods of coping with stress had lower blood pressure than those who used negative methods. Men were especially likely to use bad methods such as eating unhealthy foods, drinking more alcohol, and taking aspirin and other painkillers. Women, on the other hand, were more likely to get more exercise, laugh at their problems, and have positive outlooks on their situations. Not surprisingly, the women had lower blood pressure than the men.

It's too early to say exactly which positive methods you should use when faced with high stress. There's just not enough evidence out there yet. But you already know which methods are lousy, such as drinking and overeating.

So it can't hurt to take a serious look at yourself and figure out how you can better deal with the stress in your life.

Doctors are trying to find out whether relaxation techniques such as meditation can help lower blood pressure. It's been hit-and-miss so far. One promising study found that people with mild hypertension might get some benefit from special techniques such as deep breathing, biofeedback, and time management. In the one-year study, 73 percent of people who used a combination of these methods were able to reduce, or even to eliminate, their blood pressure medications.

Another study found that older African-American men and women got some benefit from transcendental meditation. Doctors found that meditation lowered blood pressure more than lifestyle changes did.

While all of this is promising, it's just not possible to make any solid recommendations about relaxation methods at this point. Until there's more evidence, the best you can do is try to handle stress with positive methods such as exercise and a healthy diet. Your doctor may recommend that you try meditation and similar techniques as well.

the day. One good feature of Zyban is that it can be used in combination with a nicotine patch.

Bupropion isn't for everyone. If you're already taking it for another reason, you can't increase your dose to help you quit smoking. (Another brand name for bupropion is Wellbutrin, which is used to treat depression.) And if you experience seizures or have an eating disorder such as bulimia or anorexia nervosa, Zyban isn't for you. Common side effects from Zyban include dry mouth and insomnia.

Do these treatments really help? You bet. One study looked at how successful people were when they used various smoking cessation methods. During a four-week period, 23 percent of people who were given placebos (pills without medication) managed to stay smoke-free. About 36 percent of those using the nicotine patch alone made it. About 49 percent, or nearly half, of those who took bupropion were successful. And 58 percent of people—nearly 6 in 10—who combined the patch with bupropion stayed away from cigarettes. These are very encouraging numbers.

Of course, you can't chew gum, wear patches, or take pills forever. Sooner or later, you'll need to wean yourself off them. That's why you have to add another layer to your program: a support group. There are millions and millions of Americans out there struggling to quit smoking, just like you. Many people find it much easier to handle things when they have other people with whom they can share their experiences.

The American Lung Association is a terrific resource. Call your local chapter and ask for information on support groups and other programs you can join. The association also offers lots of manuals, videos, and audiotapes that can help make you a nonsmoker for good. For more information on how to contact the American Lung Association, see Appendix 1 on page 173.

So now you've added exercise and other goodies to your arsenal against high blood pressure. Remember that the best way to make these changes is a little bit at a time. Adding too many things to your lifestyle at once can be confusing and counterproductive. There's no sense in getting burned out in a matter of months. Dealing with hypertension needs to be a lifelong process.

Now we're going to put into place the final piece of the puzzle: medication. Even with improved lifestyles, some people need medicine to make a dent in their blood pressure readings. Fortunately, blood pressure medication has come a long way over the years. You and your doctor should be able to find a drug that will do the job with few or no side effects, causing as little interruption to your life as possible.

CHAPTER 5

A Strong Defense: Medication

Remember how easy it used to be to treat a headache? You'd open a bottle of aspirin, take two tablets, and wait for the medicine to kick in.

These days, you can get a migraine just trying to pick the right pill. There's aspirin, buffered aspirin, acetaminophen, ibuprofen, and naproxen, to name just a few. And they come in dozens of brand names, doses, and forms. While the medicine is better than ever, sometimes sorting out what's right for you can be tough.

It's the same way with medicine for high blood pressure. A few years ago, you and your doctor had a choice of one or two types. Today, there are no fewer than nine classes of medication—and each comes in different brand names and subtypes and in a variety of doses. Picking the right type and dose can seem like a confusing process. But it's a vital part of your treatment.

If your doctor decides that you need to start taking medication, it's very important that you understand what it's supposed to do, why you're taking it, and what side effects you might expect. That way, you and your doctor can work together to get your blood pressure under control as quickly as possible, with the fewest possible problems.

Make no mistake about it: medicine works. Researchers believe that hypertension drugs have saved the lives of more than one million people since 1980 alone. That's the kind of statistic that should make your medicine a little easier to swallow.

WHICH PILL DOES WHAT?

If you have Stage 1 hypertension (with systolic pressure between 140 and 159 mm Hg or diastolic pressure between 90 and 99 mm Hg), your doctor might not prescribe any medication at first. That's because lifestyle changes such as a better diet, more exercise, and losing weight might by themselves be enough to do the trick. There's no point taking medicine unless you have to. In fact, your doctor may decide to wait several months to see how you react to your new eating and exercise routine.

This doesn't apply to everyone. If your blood pressure is already at Stage 2 or higher, you'll probably start medication right away. In some cases, you might even start taking more than one type of medicine at once. With advanced cases of hypertension, there's no time to fool around. You've got to lower your blood pressure before your body suffers any ill effects.

Some people with Stage 1 hypertension might need medication right away, too. When your doctor first diagnoses high blood pressure, he will run a series of tests to see if there has been any damage to your body from the elevated pressure. If he finds a problem—especially if there's trouble with your heart, blood vessels, kidneys, or eyes—you'll need

HOW BLOOD PRESSURE DRUGS WORK

Blood pressure medications work in many different places in the body. Here's a brief description of how each major class of drugs does its job:

Peripheral-acting Andrenergic Agonists block the release of adrenaline and noradrenaline from nerves. They also deplete the stores of these hormones in body tissues. This helps blood vessels widen.

Central Alpha Agonists interfere with nerve signals in the brain that cause arteries to constrict.

Alpha-Blockers block nerve impulses that trigger small blood vessels to constrict.

Beta-Blockers slow down the heart and reduce the force of the heartbeat.

Diuretics increase the amount of water and sodium that your kidneys flush from the body. This reduces the overall blood volume.

ACE Inhibitors prevent formation of angiotensin II. This hormone causes blood vessels to constrict. **Angiotensin II Receptor Blockers** block the action of the angiotensin II.

Calcium Channel Blockers prevent calcium from passing through cell membranes in the heart and in the muscle cells that surround blood vessels. This helps blood vessels widen. Some of these medicines also slow down the heart rate and cause the heart to pump less forcefully.

Direct Vasodilators relax the smooth muscles in artery walls. This allows the arteries to widen.

to go on medication immediately. The same may hold true if you have diabetes, high cholesterol, or another problem. In fact, many doctors suggest drug therapy for people with high-normal blood pressure if they have diabetes, heart failure, or kidney disease. Remember: Hypertension is serious business. Sometimes you need to take serious measures to bring it under control.

Let's take a minute to review how blood pressure works. That way, you'll have a better idea of how the different medications affect you.

Three main structures control blood pressure: your heart, your kidneys, and your blood vessels. Your heart can pump faster and harder to raise pressure, and slower and softer to lower it. Your kidneys control how much fluid is in the bloodstream. The more fluid, the higher your blood pressure. Finally, your arteries and veins can contract to raise pressure, or dilate to lower it.

High blood pressure medications work on one or more of these areas. Some reduce the force of the heartbeat. Others cause the kidneys to excrete more salt and fluid through your urine. Still others relax blood vessels. All of the medications have been shown to lower blood pressure. About 50 percent of people taking medication for hypertension will lower their blood pressure to acceptable levels with one drug. And another 30 percent will get things under control by taking two medications at once.

Which drug is right for you depends on many factors: your age, race, level of physical activity, and health factors such as diabetes, heart disease, osteoporosis, and high cholesterol. Cost can also be a consideration. Some drugs, like diuretics, are relatively cheap. Others, like calcium channel blockers and ACE (angiotensin converting enzyme) inhibitors, can cost more than $100 to $200 a month.

Finally, there are side effects to consider. Every drug, be it for headaches or heart attacks, may cause side effects. High blood pressure medication is no different. Side effects range from dizziness and drowsiness to excess hair growth. You'll need to work with your doctor to weigh your options. Sometimes minor side effects are well worth it—especially if the medicine lowers your pressure from a dangerous level to a safe one.

Here's a summary of each class of high blood pressure medication. These drugs are grouped collectively under the term *antihypertensives*.

Diuretics

These are the oldest of the high blood pressure medications. The first diuretic, chlorothiazide, first became available in 1958.

Diuretics are also known as water pills or fluid pills. This is because they cause your kidneys to remove water and sodium from your bloodstream. Less water in the bloodstream means a lower volume of blood—and that means lower blood pressure. Sodium, as you may recall, acts to keep more water in the blood. So getting rid of sodium through your urine helps reduce blood volume.

There are three different types of diuretics. The first type is known as thiazides. These are the most commonly prescribed diuretics because they have several big advantages.

First, thiazides are less expensive than other antihypertensives. One hundred tablets of the thiazide diuretic called chlorthalidone, for example, has a wholesale cost of about $16.65—less than 2 cents a pill! Depending on your dose,

100 tablets could last for one to three months. Of course, unless you have a relative in the pharmacy business, you probably won't get drugs at wholesale prices. But these medications still will be very reasonable compared with other classes of drugs.

The second advantage of thiazide diuretics is they're often taken once a day, usually in small doses. This makes life much easier.

Third, and most importantly, studies show that taking appropriate doses of antihypertensives such as thiazide diuretics can prevent stroke and heart attack. In other words, they're proven medicines.

Thiazide diuretics are a good choice for people who are sensitive to the effects of sodium because the drugs flush sodium out of the body.

Some doctors also prescribe thiazide diuretics for people who have congestive heart failure. Because these drugs reduce the volume of blood, they can make it easier for the heart to do its job.

There's one major concern with thiazide diuretics, however. Some studies have shown that high doses of these drugs could increase your chances of experiencing cardiac arrest, a type of heart attack. For example, one study of 649 people with hypertension showed that those taking high doses (100 milligrams) of a thiazide diuretic were 3.6 times more likely to have heart attacks than those taking smaller doses (25 milligrams). Compared to a smaller dose, a medium-size dose (50 milligrams) raised the risk of heart attack 1.7 times. Low doses of thiazide diuretics—and most people need only low doses—do not appear to cause the same problem. Your doctor will always prescribe the lowest dose possible, even if it takes a while to find the proper amount to take each day.

The second group of diuretics is called loop diuretics. These work in much the same way as thiazide diuretics, except they're more powerful. For this reason, doctors often prefer loop diuretics for people with congestive heart failure or reduced kidney function.

The third group, potassium-sparing diuretics, is usually used in combination with either thiazides or loop diuretics. They are weaker than the other two classes of diuretics, but they have one big advantage: They help your body retain potassium. Thiazides and loop diuretics often cause the kidneys to flush too much potassium from the bloodstream. Potassium is an extremely important nutrient. Too little of it can cause problems ranging from weakness and muscle cramps to irregular heartbeat. (On the other hand, too much potassium can be hard on people who have kidney damage, so don't take supplements without first talking to your doctor.)

The same study that looked at high-dose thiazide diuretics also found that potassium-sparing diuretics can greatly reduce the chances of cardiac arrest when used in combination with thiazides. People taking a moderate dose of thiazides (50 milligrams) had 50 percent fewer instances of cardiac arrest when they added a potassium-sparing diuretic. People on low-dose thiazides (25 milligrams) had 60 percent fewer cases of cardiac arrest when they also took a potassium-sparing diuretic.

All antihypertensives may cause side effects. Side effects are different for everyone. Many people will experience none at all, while others will have one or more. Here are some of the possible side effects of diuretics.

- ◆ Thiazide and loop diuretics: overall weakness, fatigue, impotence, gout, dizziness when standing up, dehydration,

higher levels of "bad" LDL cholesterol, lower levels of "good" HDL cholesterol, lower levels of potassium, higher triglycerides, and higher blood sugar
♦ Potassium-sparing diuretics: too-high potassium levels (possibly dangerous for people with kidney disease)

Your doctor can choose from scores of diuretics, each with its own advantages and disadvantages. Here's a partial list. First is the generic name, followed by the brand name or names (most of these drugs are also available as generic, or no-name, brands). Where appropriate, the wholesale price for 100 tablets is also listed. Remember that retail prices are almost always higher.

	Cost per 100 Tablets	Lowest Dose (mg)	Highest Dose (mg)
Thiazide Diuretics			
1) bendroflumethiazide (1.25 mg)		1.25	2.5
Naturetin (10 mg)	$130.49	5	10
2) chlorothiazide (250 mg)	$6.42	250	500
Diuril	$13.96	250	500
3) chlorthalidone (50 mg)	$16.65	25	100
Hygroton	$89.05	25	100
4) hydrochlorothiazide (50 mg)	$4.89	25	100
Esidrix	$20.60	25	100
HydroDIURIL	$21.35	25	100
5) indapamide (2.5 mg)	$75.68	1.25	2.5
Lozol	$94.30	1.25	2.5

	Cost per 100 Tablets	Lowest Dose (mg)	Highest Dose (mg)
6) methylclothiazide (2.5 mg)	$8.47	2.5	5
Enduron	$44.14	2.5	5
7) trichlormethiazide (4 mg)	$6.27	2	4
Metahydrin	$77.04	2	4
Naqua	$67.50	2	4

Loop Diuretics

1) bumetanide (0.5 mg)	$27.6	3.5	2
Bumex	$31.13	.5	2
2) ethacrynic acid			
Edecrin (50 mg)	$44.13	25	50
3) furosemide (40 mg)	$5.76	20	80
Lasix	$24.98	20	80

Potassium-Sparing Diuretics

1) amiloride			
Midamor (5 mg)	$47.78	5	10
2) spironolactone (25 mg)	$8.57	2	5
Aldactone	$41.80	25	100
3) triamterene			
Dyazide (25 mg hydrochloro-thiazide, 37.5 mg triamterene)	$41.70		
Dyrenium (50 mg)	$37.10		

Generic Drugs

Let's take a moment to talk about generic drugs. As you can see from the list, they're almost always less expensive—sometimes much less expensive—than the brand-name drugs. There are a few reasons for this. First, the company that originally first developed the drug had to pay for extensive research and testing in order to get it approved. Now the company has to earn its money back. Second, the price may be high because the original company still holds exclusive rights to the drug and can charge whatever the market will bear. Third, even though the chemical content of generic and brand-name drugs is the same, they may be made in completely different ways.

There's some argument about whether generic drugs do the same work as brand-name drugs. Some health plans pay only for generic drugs, while others pay for the brand names. Before your doctor writes your prescription, be sure to ask whether a generic drug would work.

Beta-Blockers

This class of drugs, which blocks the effects of hormones called adrenaline and noradrenaline, works in an entirely different way than diuretics. Instead of reducing the volume of blood, beta-blockers work on the heart itself, making it beat less often and with less force. This lowers the pressure in your arteries.

Beta-blockers were first developed as a treatment for angina, chest pain caused by blockages in the arteries that feed the heart muscle. Only later did researchers find out how useful these drugs can be for high blood pressure. In fact, beta-blockers are a great choice if you've already had a heart attack. Studies show that people who take beta-blockers are less likely to suffer a second heart attack. The drugs also reduce total mortality rates, which means that heart attack victims who take beta-blockers are less likely to die of any cause than those who don't.

Unfortunately, beta-blockers don't work for everyone. While they may be great for some people who've had heart attacks, they can be very dangerous for people with heart failure. Heart failure means the heart is having trouble pumping enough blood through the arteries. Reducing the heart rate and the force of each heartbeat can make matters worse.

Beta-blockers can also be dangerous for people with asthma or emphysema. The drugs can cause other problems, too. Those with diabetes must be especially careful about beta-blockers. The drugs lower the body's response to adrenaline, the hormone that warns the body when blood sugar is dropping. This means that people with diabetes who take beta-blockers may be unaware when their blood sugar drops to dangerous levels.

Beta-blockers might also raise your triglycerides and lower your HDL cholesterol. HDL is the good cholesterol that your body uses to keep blood vessels clean. If you have high blood pressure, it's important to keep track of your cholesterol levels. Even if you aren't taking beta-blockers, expect your doctor to order routine cholesterol tests just to make sure things are okay.

In both men and women, beta-blockers can reduce sex drive. In men, these drugs sometimes cause impotence. Fatigue is another common side effect. Some people report having unusually vivid dreams while taking beta-blockers. There has been some debate about whether these drugs cause depression, too. But a recent study of more than

4,300 people suffering from depression—many of whom used beta-blockers—found no link.

The side effects may be temporary. You and your doctor have to work together to find the right beta-blocker and the right dose to meet your needs. Be sure to report any unusual or dangerous side effects immediately. But don't stop taking beta-blockers unless you first get approval from your doctor. These are powerful drugs that change the way your heart works. Stopping them abruptly can cause serious problems.

Below is a list of commonly prescribed beta-blockers. The generic name is listed first, followed by the brand name. Generics won't be available if the manufacturer still holds the patent for the drug. Typical doses are given, although the amount you need may be different. Prices listed are wholesale costs; your cost will probably be higher.

	Cost per 100 Tablets	Lowest Dose (mg)	Highest Dose (mg)
Beta-Blockers			
1) acebutolol			
Sectral (200 mg)	$105.98	200	400
2) atenolol (50 mg)	$62.61	25	100
Tenormin	$95.70	25	100
3) betaxolol			
Kerlone (10 mg)	$79.43	5	10
4) bisoprolol			
Ziac (5-6.25 mg)	$97.06	5	10
5) carteolol			
Cartrol (5 mg)	$106.18	2.5	5

	Cost per 100 Tablets	Lowest Dose (mg)	Highest Dose (mg)
6) labetalol			
Normodyne (200 mg)	$66.20	100	300
7) metoprolol (100 mg)	$66.18	50	100
Lopresor	$85.40	50	100
Toprol-XL	$72.40		
8) nadolol (80 mg)	$128.77	20	160
Corgard	$160.07	20	160
9) penbutolol			
Levatol (20 mg)	$124.10	20	20
10) pindolol (10 mg)			
Visken	$112.26	5	10
11) propranolol (80 mg)	$21.85	10	80
Inderal	$98.14	10	80
12) timolol (10 mg)			
Blocadren	$52.85	5	20

ACE Inhibitors

These drugs work by relaxing the walls of your arteries and keeping them wide open. The more relaxed the walls of your arteries, the lower your blood pressure.

As noted earlier in the chapter, ACE stands for angiotensin converting enzyme. As you may recall, angiotensin is a chemical in your bloodstream that plays an important role in controlling blood pressure. When your kidneys sense a need to raise blood pressure, they secrete the hormone renin into the blood. Renin seeks out angiotensinogen, a protein that is made in your liver and that also circulates through your blood. When renin and angiotensinogen meet, they combine to form angiotensin. Angiotensin flows through the bloodstream and reaches the lungs, where it gets converted into angiotensin II. This powerful substance then signals the blood vessels that it's time to tighten up and raise pressure.

ACE inhibitors short-circuit this complicated process. They help prevent renin and angiotensinogen from getting together and forming angiotensin. Without angiotensin, there won't be angiotensin II. And without angiotensin II, your blood pressure won't rise.

ACE inhibitors may cause fewer side effects than other medications, but the evidence isn't crystal clear. ACE inhibitors shouldn't affect your sex life, since they don't cause impotence or a drop in sexual desire. Some people say that their overall mood actually improves when they start taking these drugs. If you have diabetes, ACE inhibitors may even slow down kidney damage—even if you don't have high blood pressure.

The most common side effect of ACE inhibitors is a dry cough, which affects about 25 percent of people who use the drugs. Women may be three times more likely than men to experience this side effect. A study of more than 800 people with Stage 1 or Stage 2 hypertension found that 12.6 percent of women taking lisinopril developed a cough, while only 4.4 percent of men had the same problem. Interestingly, the problem was worse for nonsmokers than for smokers. (Of course, this is no excuse to smoke!)

Less common side effects include a skin rash, a change in your sense of taste, and an increase in blood potassium levels. Higher potassium levels can be dangerous, especially for people with advanced kidney damage. Your doctor will probably check your blood potassium level before and after prescribing an ACE inhibitor, to see if the drug is causing any changes.

ACE inhibitors and thiazide diuretics can be a very effective combination to lower blood pressure. But at least one study shows that switching to a low-salt diet may have the same effect as adding a diuretic. It's always best to use as few drugs as possible. Cutting back on salt could help you avoid the potential side effects of diuretics, including loss of potassium.

Because they don't usually cause fatigue, ACE inhibitors can be a good choice for people who are physically active. They're also useful for people who have high cholesterol levels, since they don't raise cholesterol as diuretics and beta-blockers do. Others who may benefit from ACE inhibitors include people with congestive heart failure, diabetes, or mild kidney problems as well as those who have already suffered heart attacks.

For African-Americans, ACE inhibitors alone are not as effective as thiazide diuretics, so they're not usually a first choice. Still, ACE inhibitors and thiazides together can be a very effective combination, even for African-Americans.

Women of childbearing age must be very careful about ACE inhibitors. These drugs can cause birth defects. If you are taking an ACE inhibitor and are thinking about becoming pregnant, talk to your doctor about switching medication. If you discover that you're already pregnant, call your doctor immediately.

Here's a list of ACE inhibitors, following their chemical names. Except for Capoten, generic versions are not available. You'll have to use a brand-name drug.

	Cost per 100 Tablets	Lowest Dose (mg)	Highest Dose (mg)
ACE Inhibitors			
1) benazepril			
Lotensin (20 mg)	$85.19	5	40
2) captopril	$65–$117		
Capoten (50 mg)	$138.70	12.5	100
3) enalapril			
Vasotec (5 mg)	$119.43	2.5	20
4) fosinopril			
Monopril (10 mg)	$77.44	10	20
5) lisinopril			
Prinivil (10 mg)	$113.95	5	40
Zestril (10 mg)	$81.29	5	40
6) quinapril			
Accupril (10 mg)	$97.84	5	40
7) ramipril			
Altace (5 mg)	$82.28	1.25	10

Angiotensin II Receptor Blockers

This is a new class of drugs that won government approval in 1995. Angiotensin II receptor blockers work on the same principle as ACE inhibitors: They relax the walls of arteries and keep blood vessels open. They just differ in where they block the renin-angiotensin-angiotensin II cycle that we talked about earlier. ACE inhibitors prevent the body from making angiotensin II altogether. Angiotensin II receptor blockers, on the other hand, allow the production of angiotensin II in the lungs. But they block its effects on blood vessels.

Clinical trials have shown that angiotensin II receptor blockers effectively reduce blood pressure. A study of 83 men and 39 women with high hypertension found that a daily 100-milligram dose of the drug losartan significantly lowered blood pressure. The decreases ranged from 9.9 to 13.2 mm Hg systolic and 6.4 to 8.5 mm Hg diastolic.

Angiotensin II receptor blockers appear to cause few side effects. In rare cases, you may get headaches or feel dizzy or fatigued. As with ACE inhibitors, pregnant women should not use angiotensin II receptor blockers. If you are a woman of childbearing age and want to have a baby, it's very important that you talk to your doctor about your blood pressure medication beforehand.

There are only three types of angiotensin II receptor blockers on the market today. None come in a generic form. In the table below, the chemical name is listed first, followed by the brand name.

	Cost per 100 Tablets	Lowest Dose (mg)	Highest Dose (mg)
Angiotensin II Receptor Blockers			
1) losartan			
Cozaar (50 mg)	$114.04	50	100
2) valsartan			
Diovan (80 mg)	$91.23	80	160
3) irbesartan			
Avapro (75 mg)	$91.23	75	300

Calcium Channel Blockers

This class of drugs also works by relaxing the walls of arteries and keeping the arteries open. The wider the opening, the lower the blood pressure. Some calcium channel blockers also work on the heart itself, either by decreasing the force of each heartbeat or by slowing down the rate of your heartbeats.

While they seem similar to ACE inhibitors, calcium channel blockers do not affect the renin-angiotensin-angiotensin II cycle.

Calcium helps control muscle tone and action. Calcium channel blockers reduce the amount of calcium that's available for use by the muscles surrounding your blood vessels. The result is relaxed, open arteries.

Many people with angina say they get relief from their chest pain when they start taking calcium channel blockers. The drugs don't cause fatigue or drowsiness, so they're often given to people who have active lifestyles. And they don't appear to raise cholesterol levels, so they may be a good choice for people who already have high cholesterol.

The side effects of calcium channel blockers are usually mild, if they appear at all. Some people report constipation, swelling of the feet, headaches, dizziness, flushing, or slow or rapid heartbeat, sometimes with palpitations.

But there's a new concern about certain calcium channel blockers. Recent research has shown that some types of these drugs, called short-acting calcium channel blockers, may increase the risk of heart attack. One study looked at 2,655 people with high blood pressure, including 623 who had suffered heart attacks. Researchers discovered that those who took short-acting calcium channel blockers had a 60 percent greater chance of suffering heart attacks than those who took either diuretics or beta-blockers instead. The effect was greatest in people who took higher doses of short-acting calcium channel blockers.

Researchers are especially worried about the short-acting version of nifedipine. Scientists looked at a group of 16 studies and found that people taking at least 60 milligrams of this drug had a higher overall death rate than those who didn't. Among those who took at least 80 milligrams of the drug, death rates were three times higher than normal. Six percent of the people taking nifedipine died, compared with 2 percent of the people who didn't take it.

These results do not apply to calcium channel blockers that were not included in the study. But because of the new evidence, the short-acting calcium channel blocker nifedipine should not be prescribed for high blood pressure.

In general, calcium channel blockers are not the first choice for people with high blood pressure. This is especially true for people who have congestive heart failure (although the drug amlodipine, which has the brand name Norvasc, appears to be an exception to the rule). Unless there's a special reason to give you a calcium channel blocker—you have high cholesterol, for example—you'll probably start with a diuretic or beta-blocker. If you don't handle these drugs well, or if they don't do the job, you might switch to a calcium channel blocker.

Here's a very important note: If you're taking a calcium channel blocker, do not stop taking it without first talking to your doctor. Stopping the drug abruptly can cause a dangerous increase in blood pressure in some people. Discuss your concerns with your doctor. The two of you may decide to switch drugs—or your doctor may put your fears to rest.

Below is a list of calcium channel blockers. The generic form is listed first, with the brand names underneath. Prices are wholesale; your cost will probably be higher. Not all drugs are available in generic form.

	Cost per 100 Tablets	Lowest Dose (mg)	Highest Dose (mg)
Short-Acting Calcium Channel Blockers			
1) diltiazem (90 mg)	$82.75	30	120
Cardizem (90 mg)	$104.75	30	120
2) isradipine			
DynaCirc (5 mg)	$87.18	2.5	5
3) nicardipine			
Cardene (20 mg)	$43.61	20	30
4) verapamil (120 mg)	$32.53		
Calan (120 mg)	$67.78	40	120
Isoptin (120 mg)	$59.80	40	120
Long-Acting Calcium Channel Blockers			
1) verapamil			
Calan SR (180 mg)	$119.72	120	240
Covera-HS (180 mg)	$106.80	180	240
Verelan (240 mg)	$138.05	120	240
2) amlodipine			
Norvasc (5 mg)	$141.99	2.5	10

	Cost per 100 Tablets	Lowest Dose (mg)	Highest Dose (mg)
3) diltiazem			
Cardizem CD (240 mg)	$184.00	120	300
Dilacor XR (240 mg)	$127.36	120	240
4) nifedipine			
Procardia XL (30 mg)	$140.34	30	90
5) felodipine			
Plendil (5 mg)	$90.50	5	10
6) nisoldipine (Sular)	$89.00	10	40

Alpha-Blockers

Like ACE inhibitors and calcium channel blockers, alpha-blockers work on the blood vessels. But alpha-blockers target mainly smaller arteries, causing them to remain relaxed and more open. This lowers resistance inside the blood vessels and helps keep blood pressure down. Alpha-blockers work by blocking nerve impulses that normally cause the smooth muscle around the arteries to constrict.

The good thing about alpha-blockers is that most people who take them don't experience serious side effects. The drugs may be of special benefit to people with high levels of LDL cholesterol, the bad cholesterol that can clog arteries. Since alpha-blockers don't make you drowsy, they can be a good choice if you're active. Older men may get a special benefit. This class of medication helps relieve bothersome symptoms from enlarged prostate glands (straining and frequent urination at night).

There are a few things to watch out for, however. In some people—especially older folks—alpha-blockers can cause light-headedness and even fainting. This happens when people stand up quickly, which can cause their blood pressure to dip sharply (a condition called orthostatic hypotension). This problem typically occurs after the first dose of the drug is taken or after the dose is increased. Fortunately, the side effect doesn't last. Other side effects may include headaches and heart palpitations.

Some people notice that alpha-blockers become less effective over time. This is because your body tries to compensate for the lower blood pressure by holding onto more salt and water. Most of the time, adding a diuretic to your alpha-blocker can take care of this problem nicely.

Here's a list of alpha-blockers. The generic name is listed first, followed by the brand name. Not all drugs are available as generics. Prices are wholesale; your cost will probably be higher.

	Cost per 100 Tablets	Lowest Dose (mg)	Highest Dose (mg)
Alpha-Blockers			
1) doxazosin			
Cardura (4 mg)	$99.72	1	8
2) labetalol*			
Normodyne (200 mg)	$66.20	100	300
3) prazosin (2 mg)	$34.65	1	5
Minipress (2 mg)	$57.67	1	5
4) terazosin			
Hytrin (2 mg)	$165.78	1	10

*This medicine is both an alpha-blocker and a beta-blocker.

Central Alpha-Agonists

These drugs work on the same principle as do alpha-blockers, but in a different location. Both types of drugs block the nerve impulses that tighten the smooth muscle surrounding blood vessels. But while alpha-blockers work directly at the blood vessels, central alpha-agonists affect the center of the nervous system—the brain. They keep the brain from sending "tighten up" signals to the arteries. One type of central alpha-agonist, clonidine, is even available in a patch you can apply to your skin—just like the patches that help people stop smoking. You can put on a patch as little as once a week and not have to worry about remembering to take your pills each day.

Side effects from central alpha-agonists can be mild at low doses and worse at moderate or high doses. And they tend to occur more frequently than with other antihypertensive medications. Side effects include drowsiness, dizziness (especially in older people), depression, anxiety, dry mouth, sleep problems, and impotence. Because of these side effects, central alpha-agonists are a second-line choice. You'll probably use these only when other medications fail to lower your blood pressure.

It's very important that you don't stop taking central alpha-agonists without first talking to your doctor. This can lead to a dangerous rise in blood pressure that can cause all sorts of problems.

Here are the central alpha-agonists available today. The generic forms are listed first, followed by the brand names. Generics are not available in all cases. Prices listed are wholesale. You'll probably pay higher prices.

	Cost per 100 Tablets	Lowest Dose (mg)	Highest Dose (mg)
Central Alpha-Agonists			
1) clonidine (0.2 mg)	$15.29	.1	.3
Catapres (0.2 mg)	$88.46	.1	.3
Catapres (patch; 12 patches of 0.1 mg each)	$96.33	TTS-1	TTS-3
2) guanabenz (4 mg)	$59.92	4	8
Wytensin (4 mg)	$79.46	4	8
3) guanfacine			
Tenex (1 mg)	$90.08	1	2
4) methyldopa (500 mg)	$39.60	125	500
Aldomet (500 mg)	$64.84	125	500

Peripheral-Acting Adrenergic Antagonists

Drugs with this long-winded name control nerve impulses and prevent blood vessels from constricting. Peripheral-acting means they work at a distance, away from the brain. They control the action of adrenaline and noradrenaline, two substances that can raise blood pressure very quickly. Two types of this medicine, guanadrel and guanethidine, make it harder for nerves to release adrenaline and noradrenaline. A third type, reserpine, simply empties tissues of these two substances. This means there's no "fuel" to tighten the arteries when nerves give the order.

Peripheral-acting adrenergic antagonists are quite powerful. They're usually given only to people with severe cases of hypertension. The good thing about them is that they can easily be combined with other medications, such as diuretics. This gives hypertension a double whammy and can really work on stubborn cases that don't respond well to other drugs. Guanadrel and guanethidine don't cause drowsiness, either. And reserpine is quite inexpensive, which is always a plus.

But there are important side effects you need to know about. Reserpine can bring on sudden, severe cases of depression. For this reason, it's not given to people with histories of depression. Guanadrel and guanethidine can cause your blood pressure to drop extremely quickly when you stand up. They can also cause rapid blood pressure dips when you exercise. And both can cause diarrhea.

Below is a list of peripheral-acting adrenergic antagonists. The generic version is listed first, followed by the brand name. Generics are not always available. Prices listed are wholesale. You'll probably have to pay more.

	Cost per 100 Tablets	Lowest Dose (mg)	Highest Dose (mg)
Peripheral-Acting Adrenergic Antagonists			
1) guanadrel			
Hylorel (10 mg)	$74.87	10	
2) guanethidine			
Ismelin (10 mg)	$60.65	10	
3) reserpine (0.25 mg)	$8.49	.1	.25
Resa (0.25 mg)	$3.00	.1	.25

Direct Vasodilators

This final class of antihypertensives also works to keep small arteries wide open. As their name suggests, these drugs work directly on the smooth muscle of the arteries, relaxing and opening up the arteries so that there's less resistance to the flow of blood.

Direct vasodilators are among the strongest of the antihypertensive medications. Unless you have very severe high blood pressure, your doctor will not choose this medication for you. Direct vasodilators cause a number of side effects. They often cause the body to retain salt and fluid, which can actually increase blood pressure. For this reason, you'll need to take a diuretic along with the direct vasodilator. These drugs can also cause a rapid heartbeat, which tends to raise blood pressure, too. So you'll typically need to take a beta-blocker or alpha-blocker as well; both of these medicines will slow down your pulse.

There are two versions of direct vasodilators: minoxidil and hydralazine. Each can cause heart palpitations and edema—swelling caused by fluid retention. Minoxidil is the stronger of the two and is often used when a person's kidneys are functioning at a low level. If the name sounds familiar, that's because minoxidil is the same drug (but a slightly different form) that can be used to help hair regrow. Not surprisingly, a major side effect of using minoxidil is unwanted hair growth. When used in high doses, hydralazine can sometimes cause a condition with symptoms similar to the disease lupus.

As you can see, direct vasodilators are serious medications and are always used as a last resort. You have to keep in mind that the most important thing you can do for your heart is to lower your blood pressure. It's almost always worth the side effects, whatever they may be.

Below are the two direct vasodilators, listed first by generic name and then by brand name. The price listed is wholesale only; you'll most likely pay more for your medication.

	Cost per 100 Tablets	Lowest Dose (mg)	Highest Dose (mg)
Direct Vasodilators			
1) hydralazine (50 mg)	$7.11	10	50
Apresoline (50 mg)	$52.24	10	50
2) minoxidil (10 mg)	$53.30	2.5	10
Loniten (10 mg)	$113.25	2.5	10

THE RIGHT DRUG FOR YOU

With all of the blood pressure medicines on the market today, picking the right one may seem a bit like rolling the dice. But the odds are very good that you'll find a drug that works well. With Stage I hypertension, you have about a 50-50 chance of controlling your blood pressure with the first medication you take. If your doctor finds the right one immediately, it will just be a matter of finding the right dose to provide the benefits with as few side effects as possible.

Sometimes you'll need to try a different drug or a combination of drugs. With very high blood pressure, patients may need three or more drugs to control it. In most cases medication will pay real health benefits. It has been proven to lower blood pressure and the risk of stroke, heart attack, heart failure, and even death.

There is a debate among doctors about which medications are best for "frontline" treatment—that is, which high

THE OLDER, THE BETTER

Older men and women appear to get even more benefit from medication than younger folks. A recent study found that for every 1,000 elderly patients with systolic readings over 160 mm Hg, high blood pressure medication prevents about 30 strokes a year. It could also reduce nonfatal heart attacks by 27 percent and overall death rates by 13 percent.

Why do antihypertensives help older people so much? Probably because senior citizens have a greater risk of cardiovascular disease to begin with. Many people have preexisting heart or blood vessel conditions that can only be made worse by high blood pressure. Treating older people for hypertension takes away a major risk factor for heart attack and stroke, and that can be a lifesaver.

The bottom line is that you're never too old to start getting treatment.

blood pressure medicines should be the first choice and which should be used only when the first choice doesn't work. Some doctors prefer to rely on the older, tried-and-true medications such as diuretics and beta-blockers, while others believe the newer drugs do the same job without causing as many side effects.

In 1993, the Joint National Committee on Detection, Evaluation, and Treatment of High Blood Pressure tried to settle the controversy. After reviewing all of the evidence from studies conducted around the world, members of the committee produced a lengthy report that laid out its findings. The committee updated its findings in 1997.

The committee recommends that beta-blockers and diuretics should be the drugs of choice for people with uncomplicated hypertension. There are a couple of reasons for this decision. First, beta-blockers and diuretics are the only two classes of drugs that have been thoroughly tested in long-term studies. A recent review of 18 long-term studies clearly showed that these drugs can prevent heart attack and stroke. The studies compared people who were taking either beta-blockers or diuretics with people who were taking placebos. Compared with placebos, beta-blockers lowered the risk of stroke by 29 percent and the risk of congestive heart failure by 42 percent. Low-dose diuretics dropped the risk of stroke by 34 percent, congestive heart failure by 42 percent, and coronary disease by 28 percent and the overall death rate by 10 percent.

Diuretics may also be the best choice for people with a condition called left ventricular hypertrophy (LVH). As you may recall, people with LVH have a greatly enlarged heart muscle. LVH occurs because high blood pressure puts extra demands on the heart. Like any muscle, the heart gets bigger when it works harder. Eventually, its size increases to a point where it has trouble doing its job properly. This can lead to a range of problems, from angina to heart attack to an irregular heartbeat.

In one important study, researchers looked at more than 1,100 men with mild to moderate hypertension. Some of the men were given the diuretic hydrochlorothiazide, some received the beta-blocker atenolol, and others were given the ACE inhibitor captopril, the central alpha-agonist clonidine, the calcium channel blocker diltiazem, or the alpha-blocker prazosin.

After a year, the researchers looked at the men who had started with the worst cases of LVH. They found that the men taking the diuretic had a 19 percent average reduction in LVH. Men taking the ACE inhibitor had a

13 percent average reduction, while those taking the beta-blocker had an 11 percent average reduction. The other drugs also reduced LVH, but the size of the decrease was not significant.

What does all of this mean? Well, although the study was limited because it didn't include women, it does suggest that diuretics may be a particularly good drug choice for people who have LVH.

There's no doubt that other medicines, such as ACE inhibitors and calcium channel blockers, lower blood pressure. But the important question about these new (and often expensive) drugs is whether they actually prevent heart attack and stroke. Except for one calcium channel blocker that isn't even available in this country, we don't have any evidence from long-term studies. While it might seem obvious that they would, it just hasn't been proven yet. Sometimes drugs can create problems that outweigh the good they do. As we mentioned earlier, there's some evidence that short-acting calcium channel blockers may increase the risk of heart attack in certain people. Since diuretics and beta-blockers have proved themselves effective in lowering the risk of premature death, the committee believes that they should be used before the untested drugs—at least in cases of uncomplicated hypertension.

The other main concern the committee has with the newer drugs is their cost. The newer drugs can be much more expensive—sometimes hundreds of dollars a month more—than diuretics and beta-blockers. If you don't have insurance that covers the cost of medication, you might be left with a choice between a cheaper drug and no drug at all.

Not all doctors agree with the committee's recommendations. In fact, calcium channel blockers and ACE inhibitors are the two most widely prescribed blood pressure medications today. Some of this has to do with marketing; drug companies heavily market their new drugs to doctors. Older drugs and generic versions don't receive the same attention. Many physicians also like the newer drugs because they believe that these drugs have fewer side effects than diuretics and beta-blockers. Still, the evidence isn't crystal clear on this point. Since as many as half of the people who take blood pressure medications stop because they don't like the side effects, this can be an important factor.

Some doctors also feel that newer drugs cause fewer problems with cholesterol, potassium, and blood sugar. It's well known, for example, that diuretics can increase your level of "bad" LDL cholesterol and decrease your level of potassium to a small extent. Correcting these problems may mean taking other medications—and that can increase the overall cost of treatment.

The type of drug you need may depend on other factors, too. African-Americans, for example, don't respond to beta-blockers as well as they do to diuretics. People with diabetes often can't take beta-blockers because the drugs can interfere with how the body senses low blood sugar. If you have diabetes or congestive heart failure, ACE inhibitors could be the best choice for you. For men with an enlarged prostate gland, an alpha-blocker may relieve prostate symptoms and control high blood pressure at the same time. And calcium channel blockers might be the best choice for physically active people.

For a list of different populations and the drugs that may work best for them, see "Preferred Drugs for Specific Populations," pages 150 and 151. In most cases, low-dose diuretics and beta-blockers are still the drugs of choice.

PREFERRED DRUGS FOR SPECIFIC POPULATIONS

Population	Preferred Drugs	Less Preferred Drugs
People under age 50	alpha-blockers, beta-blockers, ACE inhibitors	none
People over age 65	thiazide diuretics, calcium channel blockers, ACE inhibitors	central alpha-agonists
African-Americans	thiazide diuretics	beta-blockers, ACE inhibitors
Whites	beta-blockers, ACE inhibitors	none
Active people	ACE inhibitors, calcium channel blockers, alpha-blockers	beta-blockers
People with diabetes	low-dose thiazide diuretics, ACE inhibitors, central alpha agonists, alpha-blockers	high-dose thiazide diuretics, beta-blockers
People with kidney trouble	loop diuretics, ACE inhibitors, minoxidil	potassium-sparing diuretics
People with congestive heart failure	ACE inhibitors, thiazide diuretics	beta-blockers (except carvedilol), calcium channel blockers (except amlodipine)

Population	Preferred Drugs	Less Preferred Drugs
People with heart disease	beta-blockers	direct vasodilators
People who have had heart attacks	beta-blockers, ACE inhibitors	none
People with angina	beta-blockers, calcium channel blockers, alpha-blockers	none
People with osteoporosis	diuretics	none
People with high cholesterol	ACE inhibitors, calcium channel blockers, alpha-blockers	high-dose diuretics, beta-blockers
People with high triglycerides	alpha-blockers	high-dose thiazide diuretics, beta-blockers
People with asthma	none	beta-blockers
People with histories of depression	none	central alpha-agonists, beta-blockers, reserpine
People who have trouble taking medication regularly	any drug that can be taken once a day	central alpha-agonists
Men with enlarged prostates	alpha-blockers	none

Doctors may prescribe more than one blood pressure medicine at once. Sometimes this is because the combination is more effective than either drug used alone. Using drugs in combination can also help overcome the problems individual drugs can cause. For example, many drugs cause the body to retain sodium and water. So your doctor might combine one of these drugs with a diuretic, which will help remove sodium and fluid from your bloodstream.

Drugmakers often combine medications in one pill, which makes taking them more convenient. One example is the new drug Lexxel, which combines the ACE inhibitor enalapril with the long-acting calcium channel blocker felodipine. The effects of the two drugs do not change. And the side effects don't, either. The new pill just makes things a little more convenient.

Living with Side Effects

Sometimes side effects from drugs can't be avoided. This doesn't mean you should stop taking your medication. Remember, controlling your blood pressure can save your life. A little fatigue or dizziness should be well worth the benefits of lower blood pressure. Often, side effects will diminish or even go away after your body gets used to the new medication.

Here are some of the most common side effects associated with blood pressure medication—and some tips on how to handle them.

Drowsiness. This most often happens to people who take beta-blockers and central alpha-agonists. Ask your doctor if it's okay to take the medication in one dose, about a half hour before bedtime. You're going to sleep soon anyway, so a little drowsiness isn't such a bad idea.

Headaches. People who take calcium channel blockers or angiotensin II receptor blockers sometimes get headaches. Before you take any additional medication, such as aspirin or ibuprofen, check with your doctor. These drugs might interfere with your blood pressure medication.

There are lots of tricks for easing headache pain. A hot shower or bath sometimes does the job. If your headache comes from muscle tension, try taking deep breaths to relax yourself. For some people, an ice pack across the back of the neck works; just make sure you place the pack in a towel, so the cold doesn't harm your skin. Finally, try getting more exercise, which often helps prevent headaches.

Dehydration. Diuretics can make you urinate more frequently, so it's not surprising that they may dehydrate you. This is easy enough to fix. Drink eight or more glasses of liquids each day. Try to remind yourself to drink a glass after each time you urinate. If you feel particularly weak, talk to your doctor. She may decide to decrease your drug dosage to help ease your problem. In extremely hot weather, it may also be necessary to reduce the amount of diuretics that you take.

Constipation. Some people who take calcium channel blockers may develop constipation. Drinking lots of water— at least eight glasses a day—will help keep your system working smoothly. Juice works well, too. Also, try eating more high-fiber foods such as beans, wheat bran, and whole-grain cereals. If things get too bad, ask your doctor whether it's all right to take bulk laxatives or stool softeners.

Diarrhea. Peripheral-acting adrenergic antagonists and direct vasodilators can have the opposite effect of calcium channel blockers. If diarrhea gets too bad, your doctor may prescribe an antidiarrheal drug. But don't take one on your own without asking first. Sometimes two drugs can interact in dangerous ways. For a mild case of diarrhea, try drinking clear fluids until your body is back to normal.

Dry mouth. People who take central alpha-agonists sometimes get uncomfortably dry mouths. In mild cases, sucking on a piece of sugarless candy or chewing a piece of sugarless gum can help. Some people say using mouthwash gives them relief. If things get too uncomfortable, talk to your doctor about using a saliva substitute to moisten your mouth.

Urinating at night. If you're taking a diuretic, you've probably noticed that you're going to the bathroom more often than usual. This isn't such a big deal—unless it means climbing out of bed too often at night. To solve this problem, you might be able to change the time you take your medicine. If your doctor approves, try taking your pill after breakfast. People who take more than one pill should try taking the last one in the late afternoon or early evening—say, before 6:00 p.m. That way, the medicine will have a chance to do its work before you turn out the lights.

Dizziness or light-headedness. This condition is common among people who take a beta-blocker, alpha-blocker, or direct vasodilator. In some cases, people even faint occasionally. While it's not always possible to eliminate these problems, you can take steps to lessen them. Don't stand up for long periods of time, since that can reduce the flow of blood to your head. Don't drink too much alcohol. And try not to overdo it with exercise, yard work, housecleaning, or other activities. This is especially important on warm days.

Dizziness upon standing. The technical term for this is orthostatic hypotension. It's caused by a drop in blood pressure when you stand. It means your medication is working well—maybe too well when you first stand up. This is a common problem with many antihypertensive drugs, including beta-blockers, ACE inhibitors, alpha-blockers, peripheral-acting adrenergic antagonists, and direct vasodilators.

The key to dealing with this problem is to go slow. If you're sitting in a chair, very gently rise to give your body time to adjust. If you're lying down, slowly move to a seated position. Hang your feet over the edge of the bed for a minute or two, then slowly stand up.

Sensitivity to cold. Beta-blockers sometimes cause this problem. The advice is pretty obvious: Dress warmly. Make sure you cover your feet, hands, and ears, which are extra-sensitive to cool temperatures. If you're going to be in a cold place for a while, dress in layers of clothing to help retain your body heat.

Sensitivity to sunlight. Some people who take beta-blockers, diuretics, and direct vasodilators notice that they don't handle sunshine very well. This doesn't mean you have to hide in a darkened room. If you have this problem, just take precautions when you go outside. Wear a hat with a wide brim to keep the sun off your face. Buy some good sunglasses—the kind that block ultraviolet rays (UVA and UVB). Slather on some sunblock with a sun protection factor (SPF) of 15 or higher. Cover your lips with a balm that has the same SPF. And avoid standing or sitting in direct sunlight between 10:00 a.m. and 3:00 p.m., when the sun's rays are most powerful.

Loss of potassium. Some diuretics can cause you to lose too much potassium through your urine. It's always a good idea to eat foods high in potassium, such as bananas,

CAN YOU GO TOO LOW?

Everyone agrees that people with hypertension should work to lower their blood pressure. But can you take things too far? Doctors are now looking at whether dropping diastolic blood pressure below 80 mm Hg can actually do more harm than good (or vice versa).

The higher a person's blood pressure, the more likely she is to die from a heart attack. We've known this for years. Now researchers have some concern about the other end of the scale—among people with diastolic readings that drop below about 80 mm Hg. (This applies only to people who are being treated for hypertension. If you aren't, there's little reason for concern about a diastolic reading lower than 80 mm Hg.)

It's called the J-curve phenomenon because the graph looks like a J. In some (but not all) studies, a high number of events such as heart attacks occurred at the highest blood pressure levels—the top of the J—and at another small peak at the lowest blood pressure level—the "hook" of the J. In between, at the 80 to 85 mm Hg level, the rates were lowest.

No one is quite sure why this happens. Some researchers believe the reason lies within the coronary arteries, the blood vessels that feed the heart muscle. Blood flows through these arteries only during the diastolic phase of the heartbeat. So if diastolic blood pressure is too low, the heart may not get enough blood to feed itself properly. This could be especially true in cases of left ventricular hypertrophy, since an enlarged heart needs even more blood than usual.

Others think taking high doses of diuretics could disrupt your blood glucose (sugar) and potassium levels. High blood sugar and low potassium can lead to an irregular heartbeat—and possibly a heart attack.

Not every expert believes in the J-curve, however. Some think it's just an illusion. People with severe atherosclerosis, or clogging of the arteries, often develop unusually low diastolic pressure. Since atherosclerosis can greatly increase the risk of heart attack, people with this disease are more likely to die of heart attacks than others—even though their diastolic blood pressure appears "better" than before.

Doctors are trying to hash things out with more studies. But until they get an answer to the J-curve, the rule is simple: If you're being treated for high blood pressure, your doctor will probably try to lower your diastolic reading to between 80 and 85 mm Hg—but not much further. Recent evidence from the Hypertension Optimal Treatment (HOT) study supports this goal.

orange juice, potatoes, and kidney beans. There's a list of high-potassium foods on pages 68 and 69.

Don't take potassium supplements unless you first talk to your doctor. They can cause serious problems in people who have kidney trouble. If your potassium level drops too low, your doctor may decide to add a potassium-sparing diuretic to your thiazide or loop diuretic.

Tender, swollen, or bleeding gums. Calcium channel blockers can cause this problem in some people. Make sure you brush and floss your teeth every day. Don't apply too much pressure with the toothbrush, or you may make things worse. You might try gently massaging your gums each day. Talk to your dentist about the right way to do it. And while you're there, have him give your teeth a good, thorough cleaning.

Some drugs cause more serious side effects—conditions such as gout and impotence, for example. There's not much you can do by yourself to stop them. But your doctor might be able to sort things out. Remember that people can have symptoms that are unrelated to medicine. Before switching or stopping medication, most doctors will look for other reasons for your symptoms. Keep in mind that the most important thing for you right now is to get your blood pressure down to a safer level.

STICKING WITH IT

As we've seen, it may take a while to find the proper drug and dose to suit your needs. This is why you'll probably need to see your doctor on a regular basis until things get straightened out. If you have Stage 1 hypertension and show no signs of damage from high blood pressure, your doctor will want to see you a month or two after you start your medication. She'll check to see how your blood pressure has reacted to the drug you've been taking. You may need to increase the dose a little to get a better result. If the side effects are too bad, you may switch to a lower dose—or you may even try a different drug.

Your doctor will also want to know how you've been doing with your lifestyle changes. Eating better, quitting smoking, getting more exercise, and maybe even reducing stress can have a big impact on your blood pressure. In some cases, these healthy habits will allow you to take a lower dose of medication. With lower doses come fewer side effects. You might even be lucky enough to stop taking drugs altogether after a time, if you respond well enough to diet and exercise.

For people with a heart condition, kidney problems, or previous stroke or for those with blood pressure at Stage 2 or higher, the return trip to the doctor comes a little sooner.

After two to four weeks, you'll need to check back with your doctor to see how well your medication is working. You may need a stronger dose, a different drug, or a second drug to get things rolling. If you have severe hypertension, you may even need a combination of three or more drugs to get the job done.

Once you get your blood pressure under control, the office visits will come less often. Most people need to check back with their doctors every three to six months. You'll probably take a blood test to see how the drugs are affecting your body chemistry. Your doctor will need to check your sodium and potassium levels, among other things. Some antihypertensives can really throw these minerals out of balance, so it's important to keep tabs on them. In many cases, your doctor will want to check your kidney function to make sure the high blood pressure medication hasn't made things worse.

If you make major lifestyle changes—such as eating better and exercising regularly—it may be possible to stop using high blood pressure medication. This only should be done with your doctor's approval and guidance. First you have to bring your blood pressure under control for at least one full year. Your doctor will need to check your pressure at least four times during this year, since one reading isn't enough to be sure. Then—and only then—will your doctor consider tapering the drugs. Not everyone will be able to stop all medicine.

Taking Your Medicine

Despite the many advances in treating high blood pressure, only about one in four people with hypertension has lowered his blood pressure to an acceptable level. One reason for this rather disappointing number is that as many as 30 percent of people with high blood pressure don't even know they have it. But there's another reason, one that should never occur: Many people simply stop taking their medicine.

It's sort of understandable. Hypertension is one of those problems that doesn't have many symptoms. You don't usually feel bad when you have it. But when you start taking medication, you may develop side effects. So instead of feeling better when you take your pills, you may feel a little worse.

There isn't an easy answer for this. Just remind yourself that you need the medicine to bring your blood pressure down. Whether you feel it or not, hypertension causes serious damage. Consider the side effects as a sure sign that your medicine is working, and try to be happy with that.

Sometimes people simply forget to take their medicine. This is also understandable, especially if you're not used to prescriptions. The best way to handle this is to make pill-taking part of your routine. If you're supposed to take your medicine in the morning, put it on the kitchen table the night before. That way, it will be in front of you when you sit down to your cereal. If you need to take your medicine at night, put the bottle on top of your alarm clock, so you won't go to sleep without seeing it.

If you're taking medicine that requires more than one dose a day, talk to your doctor. Maybe he can change the prescription to something you need to take only once every 24 hours. Most people find that it's twice as easy to stick with the plan when they have to take only one pill a day.

Most importantly, let other people help you. Your husband isn't nagging when he asks if you've taken your medicine. He's trying to help you stay healthy. Ask for the support of your friends and family, and thank them for caring.

Treating hypertension with medicine can be complicated. But it's certainly worth whatever frustration or inconvenience you may have to put up with at first. To fight hypertension, you need to make a lifelong commitment to your health. The new foods you eat, the new activities you do, and the new medication you take will have to become part of your everyday routine. Don't worry: After a few months, it will all seem like second nature.

CHAPTER 6

Special Circumstances

In some ways, having hypertension is like having high cholesterol or being overweight: It's a condition that doesn't go away. You're going to have to deal with it for the rest of your life.

Inconvenient? Sometimes. But once you've made controlling high blood pressure part of your life—by eating well, exercising, and perhaps taking medication—it becomes automatic, like brushing your teeth in the morning. You probably won't think twice about it most days.

Every once in a while, however, a special situation will crop up. If you decide to take a trip, for example, you'll need to prepare ahead of time to make sure things go smoothly. Women have a couple of additional issues to consider, such as how hypertension may affect their pregnancies or starting hormone replacement therapy after menopause. Even simple things like getting a cold can require extra thought because mixing antihypertensives with some over-the-counter drugs can have serious side effects.

In the following pages, we'll look at some of these situations, then send you on your way with a few words of advice.

TRAVEL AND HYPERTENSION

If you're taking care of yourself, high blood pressure shouldn't put a major crimp in your lifestyle. You'll be able to hop on a cruise ship, fly around the world, or simply meet your family in Des Moines. But you'll also have to do things a little differently than if you didn't have hypertension.

Plan ahead. Before traveling, check in with your doctor. This is especially true if you're planning a challenging trip or if your blood pressure hasn't been well controlled. She'll give you some good advice about what you can and can't do. She'll also give you advice on how to keep taking your medication on schedule—even when you'll be hopping through time zones like Amelia Earhart. For longer trips, you may need to get your prescription refilled before you leave.

Watch your temperature. If you're not used to it, heat can cause your blood pressure to rise a little bit. When you're traveling to a warm area, try to stay out of the sun during the hottest parts of the day. Find a nice, air-conditioned place, such as a museum or a restaurant, and wait until things cool down a little. When you're outside, take it slowly. Give yourself plenty of breaks so that your body can recover a little. And drink plenty of water. Don't become dehydrated.

Speak the language. It's very important to know a few key phrases in the language that the locals use. "I need a doctor" is the most critical. Learn how to say "I have high blood pressure," too.

Watch out for salt. When you're on the road, high-sodium foods are everywhere. Airline and restaurant food, for example, can be very high in salt. Call the airline ahead of time and ask for a low-sodium meal. If you're in a restaurant, don't hesitate to ask questions. Maybe the chef can prepare a low-sodium version of the dish you want.

Make sure you're covered. Check your health insurance plan before you leave home. Some companies will not cover you if you become ill or have an accident outside the United States. Traveling abroad without the right coverage just isn't worth the risk.

Be prepared. Before you leave home, make a list of important health facts. Write down all of the medications you're taking, including the doses. And don't forget to list the name and phone number of your doctor. That way, any physician who needs to treat you while you're away can call your primary doctor and get the lowdown on your condition.

Mind your medication. If you think traveling is hard on you, imagine what it can do to your medicine. It gets exposed to heat and humidity. Plus, it could end up in Brazil with your lost baggage while you walk around in Hawaii wearing yesterday's clothes.

It's a good idea to carry two full supplies of your medication. Keep one with you, and put the other one in your luggage. This way, you'll be sure that at least one of them makes it to your destination.

By the way, always leave your pills in their original bottles. Customs agents are understandably suspicious. You can avoid unnecessary problems at the airport by keeping things simple.

Have your doctor give you an extra written prescription for your medication, too. Be sure he includes the generic name for your drug. If you're traveling to a foreign country, the pharmacists might not recognize or carry your particular brand. But they'll probably have the generic version handy.

Treat your medication like a privileged passenger. Keep the original cotton in the bottle. This keeps the pills from shifting around and breaking. And keep your pills in a cool, dry, dark place whenever you can. That's because some pills can lose their potency when they are exposed to the elements.

One last note about medication: If you're going on a high-altitude trip, ask your doctor if she needs to change your dose. Some drugs are less effective at elevations of 6,000 feet and higher. If you're taking a diuretic to control your hypertension, you may need to take along an extra potassium supplement.

FOR WOMEN ONLY

Women with high blood pressure have a few more issues to consider than men. Most of these issues revolve around the reproductive system and hormones. For instance, does taking birth control pills affect your blood pressure?

Well, a few years ago, there might have been a problem. The old-style pills, which used high doses of estrogen to control the menstrual cycle, did cause high blood pressure in about 5 percent of the women who took them. Today, though, the estrogen-based pills have fallen out of favor. They've been replaced by low-dose pills that contain little or no estrogen.

There are two main types of birth control pills: mono-phasic and multiphasic. Studies have shown that women who take the monophasic variety (such as Ovral, Ovcon-35 and 50, Norlestrin 2.5/50 and 1/50, Demulen 1/35 and 1/50, Loestrin 1.5/30 and 1/20, and Lo Ovral) may have very slight increases in blood pressure. But the rise is not significant and seems to pose no danger. Multiphasic birth control pills (such as Ortho-Novum 7/7/7 and 10/11, Jenest, Tri-Norinyl, Tri-Cyclen, and Triphasil) have not been shown to raise blood pressure levels at all.

The bottom line? If you have hypertension, it's probably all right for you to take birth control pills. But you'll need

PREGNANCY AND HYPERTENSION

Thinking about having a baby? Great! Women with high blood pressure usually have no complications during pregnancy and give birth to healthy children. But there may be a few additional risks, so you'll need to plan ahead.

High blood pressure occurs in about 1 of every 10 pregnancies. There are four types of hypertension that may affect you.

Primary hypertension. This is the most common type of hypertension—the one we've been talking about throughout this book. You don't get hypertension just because you're having a baby. Experts believe that 1 to 5 percent of all women who become pregnant had blood pressure readings at or above the 140/90 mm Hg level before their pregnancies.

There's not much your doctor will do in cases of mild to Stage 1 hypertension. If your diastolic blood pressure remains under 100 mm Hg, your doctor may decide to keep you off blood pressure medication until you have your baby. This makes sense, since diastolic pressure usually drops 7 to 10 mm Hg during the first two trimesters of pregnancy.

If you're currently taking an ACE inhibitor or an angiotensin II receptor blocker, your doctor will need to change your prescription. ACE inhibitors can cause birth defects, particularly if taken during the second or third trimester. No other class of blood pressure medication seems to cause these problems. Doctors often prescribe methyldopa, a central alpha-agonist, for pregnant women. It has been used successfully in pregnant women for decades. Long-term studies have shown that children born to mothers who were taking methyldopa did perfectly well.

Your doctor may advise you to get as much bed rest as possible. Studies have shown that this can reduce your chances of a premature delivery and lower your blood pressure—maybe to the point where you won't need to take medication during your pregnancy. (Pregnant women naturally urinate more often; this may also help keep blood pressure down.) Bed rest doesn't mean lying down for nine months. But you should try to plan things so that you can spend as much time off your feet as possible.

Preeclampsia. This is the second type of hypertension that may occur during pregnancy. It can be much more serious than primary hypertension. Preeclampsia can lead to severe swelling and kidney or liver damage in the mother—and can threaten the health of the fetus as well. Signs of preeclampsia include a sudden rise in blood pressure to 160 mm Hg or more systolic, or 110 mm Hg or more diastolic; a high level of protein in the urine; fluid retention; stomach pain; headaches; and changes in laboratory tests. Preeclampsia usually occurs after the first 20 weeks of pregnancy.

Researchers believe that 10 to 20 percent of pregnant women will develop preeclampsia. Women having their first children are at much higher risk, as are those carrying twins. And if other women in your family have developed preeclampsia, you're more likely to get it, too.

Preeclampsia can lead to eclampsia—seizures that are a leading cause of death among pregnant women. We're not trying to scare you here. But you need to be aware of this serious, but fortunately uncommon, problem. If you are at high risk for developing preeclampsia, it's vital that you see your doctor on a regular basis. You may be asked to monitor your blood pressure at home during your pregnancy, just to keep tabs on things between doctor visits.

Preeclampsia superimposed upon essential hypertension. Women who have high blood pressure before they become pregnant are no more or less likely to develop preeclampsia than other women. But if you do have high blood pressure and then develop preeclampsia, it could threaten your pregnancy. This is the third type of hypertension.

By themselves, essential hypertension and preeclampsia may increase your chances of a problem pregnancy. Together, they can cause very serious—even to the point of life-threatening—trouble. That's why we can't stress this enough: See your doctor on a regular basis during pregnancy.

Transient hypertension. Not all types of high blood pressure during pregnancy are dangerous. The fourth type, called transient hypertension, occurs when your blood pressure rises above a normal level during pregnancy and then falls after your baby is born. Women with this condition do not have any symptoms of preeclampsia-eclampsia. Transient hypertension does not usually cause problems during pregnancy.

If you do develop transient hypertension, your risk of getting hypertension later in life is somewhat higher. So take it as an early warning—and take steps to keep your blood pressure under control.

to pay close attention to your blood pressure. If you're taking medication other than diuretics for high blood pressure, ask your doctor whether you should switch. Diuretics can help reduce the swelling that sometimes occurs in women taking birth control pills.

Hormone replacement therapy is popular among older women. When some women reach menopause, they begin taking estrogen to stop hot flashes and other types of menopausal discomfort and to prevent osteoporosis and possibly heart disease. Fortunately, hormone replacement therapy doesn't raise blood pressure. So if you're taking estrogen for other health reasons, having high blood pressure shouldn't get in the way of your treatment.

DON'T MIX YOUR MEDICINES

When you get a headache or a sore back, you probably don't think twice about popping a couple of Advil. Well, you're going to have to be a little more careful if you're taking medication to control high blood pressure. This is because a number of prescription and over-the-counter medicines can keep your blood pressure medication from doing its job.

Be sure to talk to your doctor about all of the medications you take. He'll be able to tell you whether there's going to be a problem. Usually, it's something you can solve by switching blood pressure medications or altering your dose.

Here are some of the prescription drugs that can raise your blood pressure or interfere with your antihypertensive medication.

- Nonsteroidal anti-inflammatory drugs such as indomethacin (brand name Indocin), ibuprofen (brand name Motrin), and many others
- Cyclosporine (brand name Sandimmune)
- Adrenal corticosteroids such as prednisone
- Colestipol (brand name Colestid)
- Cholestyramine (brand name Questran)
- Antidepressants such as amitriptyline (brand name Elavil) and phenelzine (brand name Nardil)
- Naloxone (brand name Narcan)
- Epoetin (brand names Epogen, Procrit)
- Rifampin (brand name Rimactane)

Note: Neither colestipol nor cholestyramine will interfere with your blood pressure medication unless you take it at the wrong time of day. Be sure to talk to your doctor or pharmacist about taking your medicines at the proper times to ensure that they both work well.

Now here's a brief list of over-the-counter medicines that may cause problems with your blood pressure medication. Again, it's very important that you speak with your doctor about the medicines you keep around the house for headaches, allergies, or weight loss.

- Nonsteroidal anti-inflammatory drugs such as ibuprofen (brand name Advil), ketoprofen (brand names Orudis or Actron), and naproxen (brand name Naprosyn)
- Nasal decongestants such as Dristan, Sine-Aid, and Sudafed
- Diet pills such as Acutrim and Dexatrim
- Any substance that contains licorice (including chewing tobacco)

Please note that these are not complete lists. With the thousands of drugs on the market today, it's impossible to list all of the potentially hazardous combinations. So don't take chances. Take a complete list of medications with you the next time you see your doctor.

LIVE A LITTLE!

Hypertension is a serious disease. But fortunately, it's a treatable one. If you take the advice in this book to heart—and listen to what your doctor says—things are almost certainly going to be all right.

You now know that you'll have to play an active role in beating high blood pressure. Medication will help, but no magic pill is going to make the problem disappear. It's going to take some old-fashioned hard work on your part. You'll have to make some changes—break some old habits and start some new ones. You'll need to remain vigilant. But the payoff is big. With your blood pressure under control, you can live a long, healthy life.

Go ahead, make the effort. You're worth it.

APPENDIX 1

For More Information

If you're looking for more information on hypertension and related topics or medical conditions, here are a few places to start.

ORGANIZATIONS

American College of Cardiology
9111 Old Georgetown Road
Bethesda, MD 20814-1699
Phone: (800) 253-4636
(301) 897-5400
Internet: *www.acc.org*

This is a professional medical society that offers several publications, sponsors programs to further medical education, maintains a national clinical database library, and advises on health care policy.

American Heart Association
7272 Greenville Avenue
Dallas, TX 75231-4596
Phone: (800) 242-8721
(214) 373-6300
Internet: *www.amhrt.org*

This national organization offers an abundance of heart-related information, pamphlets, and other resources to the public. It also sponsors public education programs. The Internet site offers a wide variety of information, from breaking news to heart quizzes to hundreds of articles on diet, nutrition, exercise, and more.

American Lung Association
Phone: (800) LUNG-USA
Internet: *www.lungusa.org*

The association offers free general information on smoking cessation. It also sells videotapes and smoke-ending programs. The Internet site is a good source of statistics, tips, programs, and support groups.

Citizens for Public Action on Blood Pressure and Cholesterol
P.O. Box 30374
Bethesda, MD 20824
Phone: (301) 770-1711
Fax: (301) 770-1713

This is a public-interest group that offers information on blood pressure and cholesterol. Write or fax the group for details.

Hypertension Network
Internet: *www.bloodpressure.com*

This Internet site offers basic and advanced information on high blood pressure to the general public. Features include a glossary of terms, a question-and-answer section, and summaries of new research on hypertension, including the effects of lifestyle changes and diet.

National Heart, Lung, and Blood Institute Information Center
P.O. Box 30105
Bethesda, MD 20824-0105
Phone: (800) 575-WELL
(301) 251-1222
Internet: *www.nhlbi.nih.gov*

This is a branch of the National Institutes of Health. It offers the public written information on all heart-related topics, including hypertension.

National High Blood Pressure Education Program
Internet: *www.nhlbi.nih.gov/nhlbi*

This program is a cooperative venture between the National Heart, Lung, and Blood Institute (see address above) and a great number of voluntary and professional health organizations. The Internet site features basic information on preventing and controlling high blood pressure. It also offers a great variety of publications for the public and professionals.

National Stroke Association
96 Inverness Drive East, Suite I
Englewood, CO 80112-5112
Phone: (303) 649-9299

Fax: (303) 649-1328
E-mail: info@stroke.org
Internet: *www.stroke.org*

This is a national health care organization that focuses on stroke prevention, treatment, rehabilitation, research, and support for stroke survivors and their families. The group's Internet site offers a list of publications, membership information, locations of regional support groups, and more.

SUPPORT GROUPS

The Coronary Club
Cleveland Clinic Foundation EE37
9500 Euclid Avenue
Cleveland, OH 44195
Phone: (800) 478-4255
(216) 444-3690
Internet: *www.heartline-news.org*

This is a national organization that is open to everyone. It focuses on keeping your heart healthy. The club publishes a monthly newsletter and offers discount prices on products that improve your cardiac health.

Mended Hearts
7272 Greenville Avenue
Dallas, TX 75231-4596
Phone: (214) 706-1442
Internet: *www.mendedhearts.org*

This is a heart disease support group sponsored by the American Heart Association. Designed for heart patients and their families, Mended Hearts has more than 250 chapters in the United States. Call or write for more information or for a referral to a chapter near you.

Electric Home Blood Pressure Monitors

In 1996, *Consumer Reports* magazine rated a number of electronic home blood pressure monitors. Here's a summary of the findings.

AND UA-767. Price: $80.
Recommendation: Excellent, if somewhat noisy.
Comments: Arm cuff, four AA batteries, self-inflating. Two-year warranty for materials and workmanship. Top-notch in accuracy and consistency. Easy to use with a large display and clear, large-print instructions. A switch lets you preset the inflation level, and you can adjust the rate of deflation. A different cuff size can be ordered for an additional charge. But it's noisier than most and lacks a storage case.

Omron HEM-711. Price: $90.
Recommendation: Very good overall, but pricey.
Comments: Arm cuff, four AA batteries, self-inflating. One-year warranty on materials and workmanship. Excellent accuracy and very good consistency. Cuff has a marker to help you place

it properly on your arm. Different cuff sizes are available at additional cost. Has an AC adapter jack; adapter must be bought separately from the company. It has no storage case.

AND UA-702. Price: $45.
Recommendation: Very good. Though basic, it has the essentials—accuracy, consistency, and good value. A *Consumer Reports* Best Buy.
Comments: Arm cuff, four AA batteries, manual inflation. Two-year warranty on materials and workmanship. Excellent accuracy and very good consistency. Instruction booklet is thorough and has large print. Rate of cuff deflation can be adjusted. Different cuff sizes are available at additional cost. It has no storage case.

Omron HEM-712C. Price: $60.
Recommendation: Very good. It is fully automatic, gets high marks on performance, and has a reasonable price tag.
Comments: Arm cuff, four AA batteries, self-inflating. One-year warranty on materials and workmanship. Excellent accuracy and very good consistency. Has memory recall of the last pressure reading. Has a switch for preset inflation levels; for higher levels, press the Start button until it reaches the pressure you want. A tab on the cuff helps with proper placement on your arm. Different cuff sizes are available for additional cost. Equipped with an AC adapter jack; adapter must be purchased separately from the company. Lacks a storage case.

Lumiscope 1085M. Price: $90.
Recommendation: A very good performer, but pricey.
Comments: Arm cuff, four AA batteries, self-inflating. One-year warranty on materials, workmanship, and accuracy. Excellent accuracy and good consistency. The display is the largest of all tested models. You can preset the inflation levels electronically by pressing a button. Provides reading of last pressure taken. Comes with storage pouch.

Sunbeam 7652. Price: $65.
Recommendation: Performs well, but may cause some discomfort.
Comments: Arm cuff, four AA batteries, self-inflating. One-year warranty on materials and workmanship. Accuracy is very good; consistency is good. Displays the last pressure reading. Inflation level can be preset electronically. Comes with a hard, protective case. Rigid material at the edges of the cuff may pinch your skin. Some samples had a slow deflation rate, which can cause discomfort.

Walgreens 91. Price: $65.
Recommendation: Works well.
Comments: Arm cuff, four AA batteries, self-inflating. One-year warranty on materials and workmanship. Very good accuracy and good consistency. A tab on the cuff helps you place it properly on your arm. Different cuff sizes are available at additional cost. Equipped with an

AC adapter jack; adapter must be purchased from the company. It has no storage case.

Omron HEM-412C. Price: $50.

Recommendation: Works well, but lacks the convenience of self-inflating cuff.

Comments: Arm cuff, four AA batteries, manual inflation. One-year warranty on materials and workmanship. Very good accuracy and good consistency. A tab on the arm cuff helps with proper placement. Different cuff sizes available at additional cost. Lacks a storage case.

Lumiscope 1065. Cost: $54.

Recommendation: Lacks the quality and convenience of other monitors. There are better choices.

Comments: Arm cuff, nine-volt battery, manual inflation. One-year warranty on materials, workmanship, and accuracy. Accuracy is good and consistency is fairly good. Memory holds last pressure reading. It lacks a storage case.

Sunmark 144. Cost: $40.

Recommendation: There are better choices.

Comments: Arm cuff, nine-volt battery (included), manual inflation. One-year warranty on materials and workmanship. Good accuracy; fair consistency. Tab on the arm cuff helps with proper placement. Different cuff sizes available. Monitor kit comes with digital thermometer. Lacks a storage case.

Sunbeam 7622. Price: $40.
Recommendation: There are better choices.
Comments: Arm cuff, four AA batteries, manual inflation. One-year warranty on materials, workmanship. Fair accuracy and consistency. Memory holds last reading. A hard, protective case. But rigid material cuff edges may pinch your skin. Some samples had a slow deflation rate, which can cause discomfort.

Omrom HEM-605. Price: $110.
Recommendation: Very good, the best of the wrist-cuff models.
Comments: Wrist cuff, two AAA batteries (included), self-inflating. One-year warranty on materials and workmanship. Very good accuracy and good consistency. Easy to use. It's uniquely light-weight and compact: Processor sits atop the cuff like a large wristwatch. Comes with hard, protective case.

Omron HEM-601. Price: $100.
Recommendation: Performs well; easy to use.
Comments: Wrist cuff, four AA batteries (included), self-inflating. One-year warranty on materials and workmanship. Very good accuracy and consistency. Easy to use and read, with large, clear display. Has switch to select preset inflation level; pressing Start button lets you choose a higher pressure. Comes with a hard, protective case for cuff and tubing.

Lumiscope 1090. Price: $110.

Recommendation: Acceptable performance and lots of features, but there are better wrist monitors.

Comments: Wrist cuff, four AA batteries, self-inflating. One-year warranty on materials, workmanship, accuracy. Fair accuracy and fair consistency. Diagram on wrist cuff helps with proper placement. Easy-to-follow instructions printed on lid of the monitor housing. Memory can store 28 blood pressure and pulse readings for one person or 14 readings for two; time and date also recorded. Comes with inflatable pad to help position wrist at heart level. A protective shell encases the monitor.

AND UB-325. Price: $125.

Recommendation: Offers many features and acceptable performance, but there are better monitors.

Comments: Wrist cuff, four AA batteries, self-inflating. Two-year warranty for materials and workmanship. Accuracy and consistency are fair. Diagram on wrist cuff helps with proper placement. Booklet instructions are in large print; instructions are also provided on the lid of the monitor housing. Memory can store time, date, and 28 pressure and pulse readings for one person or 14 readings for two people. Provides inflatable armrest to position wrist at heart level. A protective shell encases the monitor.

Omron HEM-806F. Price: $160.
Recommendation: Not acceptable. Did not give
reliable results.
Comments: Finger cuff, two AA batteries (included),
self-inflating. Performance was never better
than fair, and sometimes worse. Often gave
wrong measurement without providing an
error message.

AND UB-211. Price: $110.
Recommendation: Not acceptable. Did not give
reliable results.
Comments: Finger cuff, two AA batteries, self-
inflating. Accuracy and consistency are poor.
Monitor often gave wrong reading without
providing an error message.